Multiple Genres, Multiple Voices

Also in the CrossCurrents series

Attending to the Margins

Coming of Age

Coming to Class

Composition, Pedagogy, and the Scholarship of Teaching

Conflicts and Crises in the Composition Classroom

The Dissertation and the Discipline

Feminist Empirical Research

Foregrounding Ethical Awareness in Composition and English Studies

Getting Restless

Good Intentions

Grading in the Post-Process Classroom

Gypsy Academics and Mother-Teachers

Kitchen Cooks, Plate Twirlers, and Troubadours

Know and Tell

Latino/a Discourses

Life-Affirming Acts

Miss Grundy Doesn't Teach Here Anymore

The Mythology of Voice

Outbursts in Academe

The Politics of Writing Centers

The Politics of Writing in the Two-year College

The Profession of English in the Two-year College

Race, Rhetoric, and Composition

Resituating Writing

Rhetoric and Ethnicity

A Rhetoric of Pleasure/Sentimental Attachments

Textual Orientations

The War Against Grammar

A Way to More

Writing in an Alien World

Multiple Genres, Multiple Voices

Teaching Argument in Composition and Literature

Cheryl L. Johnson and Jayne A. Moneysmith

New Perspectives in Rhetoric and Composition

CHARLES I. SCHUSTER, SERIES EDITOR

Boynton/Cook Publishers, Inc.
HEINEMANN
Portsmouth, NH

Boynton/Cook Publishers, Inc.
A subsidiary of Reed Elsevier Inc.
361 Hanover Street
Portsmouth, NH 03801–3912
www.boyntoncook.com

Offices and agents throughout the world

Library of Congress Cataloging-in-Publication Data
Johnson, Cheryl.
  Multiple genres, multiple voices : teaching argument in composition and literature / Cheryl Johnson and Jayne Moneysmith.
    p. cm.
  ISBN 0-86709-547-4   (acid-free paper)
  1. English language—Rhetoric—Study and teaching—United States.   2. English philology—Study and teaching—United States.   3. Report writing—Study and teaching—United States.   4. Persuasion (Rhetoric)—Study and teaching.   5. Literary form—Study and teaching.   I. Moneysmith, Jayne.   II. Title.
  PE1405.U6J64 2005
  808'.042'071—dc22   2004028013

Editor: Charles Schuster
Production coordinator: Sonja S. Chapman
Production service: TechBooks
Cover design: Night and Day Design
Compositor: TechBooks
Manufacturing: Steve Bernier

Printed in the United States of America on acid-free paper
09 08 07 06 05 DA 1 2 3 4 5

Contents

Acknowledgments
vii

Foreword by Bruce Ballenger
ix

One
Multivoiced Argument: A New View
1

Two
How to Write the Multivoiced Argument
11

Three
Shorter Multivoiced Assignments
31

Four
**Reading, Revising, and Evaluating the
Multivoiced Argument**
41

Five
Reflections and Sources for Further Learning
51

References
57

Appendix A
**Two Capstone Multivoiced Arguments
and Supporting Materials**
59

Assignment Sheet for MVA Capstone
59

"Rationale" Form
60

Jen's "The Feminine Ideal: Women in the Media"
62

Melanie's "Gilead Revisited: A Contemporary
Tale of Censorship in America"
89

Acknowledgments

On the day we began thinking about what to say on our acknowledgments page, we came home to find the issue of *College English* containing a tribute to Wendy Bishop. One of Bishop's comments to another teacher particularly moved us because it expresses exactly how we feel about our book: "doesn't everyone understand that most books fail, get remaindered fast, never match their promise. It's the writing them that sets loose energy in the universe."

Writing books sets loose energy in the universe. . . .

How like Wendy to articulate precisely an idea that was vaguely swimming through our heads. For it was that intangible but very real *energy* that sustained us through the long process of writing this book. How appropriate, too, that this comment we found on the day we finished the book should come from Wendy Bishop. For, though many in the field have influenced us, without her this book may never have happened. After reading our chapter on multigenre writing and research she had solicited for her book *The Subject is Research*, she suggested that we write a book and told us—quite correctly—that Heinemann would be the best publisher to work with.

We also thank the many students at the University of Idaho and Kent State University Stark Campus whose successes, failures, and candid self-reflection helped us refine our ways of teaching multivoiced and multigenre arguments. We are grateful to students who contributed their papers to the book's Web site. We are especially indebted to Jen Eliopulos (whose work ethic and patience inspire us) and to Melanie Cattrell (there will never be another Melanie), each of whose full-length multivoiced projects appear in Appendix A of this book. Did we teach them, or did they teach us?

Samuel Johnson once said that "inspiration strikes when the printer's boy is in the hall." Without Jayne's young boys, Jackson and Jacob, playing at her side as she feverishly works on drafts, or Cheryl's grown children—Brendan, Suzanne and Steve—and grandchildren—Brittnee, Ashley and CJ—entering her life at critical points in the drafting process, we'd never have been able to write with such intensity and care. We especially want to thank our husbands, Brent and Bill, for their support and humor. They know how to listen, cook wonderful meals (some delivered to our desks), clean, and offer sound editorial advice. Some debts truly are too deep to express in words.

Jayne would like to thank her colleagues at Kent State Stark, particularly Dean William Bittle and Associate Dean David Baker for their approval of a course release during the writing of the proposal and first draft.

At the University of Idaho, Cheryl acknowledges Dr. Douglas Adams and Dr. David Barber for their unflagging support of her project and her teaching, Dr. Candida Gillis for her collaborative spirit and sharing of her expertise; and Elinor Michel, Director of the Northwest Inland Writing Project, for her mentoring.

Jayne and Cheryl appreciate Dr. Gordon Thomas' support and friendship throughout this process. He chaired our first CCCC session on multivoiced argument and will be at our first signing of our book.

We'd also like to thank Charles Schuster, our editor, for his enthusiastic support, his eye for clarity, and his attention to detail, and the excellent editorial and production staff at Boynton/Cook Heinemann.

Finally, each of us would like to thank her coauthor, though "collaboration" hardly reveals the layers and depths of our intertwined lives. We will always be grateful for our friendship, one woven tightly with words, late night emails, and mutual respect. As our writing neared completion, it became apparent that three entities wrote this book: Cheryl, Jayne, and *us*. It was the *us* that made it all worthwhile.

Foreword

In the 100 plus years since the research paper—or "source theme"—was first introduced as a distinct genre of student writing, the assignment has been driving people nuts. "Let's talk about the research paper," writes one college instructor as she introduces this subject to her readers in a journal article, " . . . granted, a dispiriting proposal. But although it bores everybody damn near to death, a great many college courses . . . have a RESEARCH PAPER embedded in them like a stone. And we all hate it." Much of the scholarship on teaching the assignment begins with a similar apology, complaint, or tale of woe. Of course, students, when asked, have their own familiar odious views of the research paper. They see it as a rite of passage, a form of punishment, the kind one endures because it's supposed to be good for you.

This is a view shared by many of their instructors. It was certainly mine for many years, until I detected something seriously wrong with the research papers my students wrote for me. It wasn't that they were boring, though they often were. It wasn't that they were written, as one of my colleagues put it, as if "there was no one home." No, what really bothered me was that they were an empty performance, much like the musical in which my daughter appeared at Camp Crescendo this summer that featured corny music about how wonderful it was to be at Camp Crescendo. Everybody dutifully sang, but with every word they began to realize they believed none of it. For many students, academic writing inspires a similar lack of conviction. Writing a research paper, one student told me, is like "an atheist going to church."

Over the years, instructors reacted to this problem in different ways. In the fifties, there was something called the "controlled research paper." Publishers churned out books on mostly famous authors or canonical texts that contained all the research a student might need—essays by experts, reviews, interviews, profiles—and students simply dined at the buffet they provided, writing their papers without a trip to the library. In the sixties, there was a move to abolish the research paper altogether from composition courses. In the seventies, Ken Macrorie led a minor revolution and proposed something called the "I-Search" paper, an alternative to the conventional research paper that still enjoys a loyal following. Though the traditional, argumentative, thesis-support research paper still holds sway in writing textbooks, the last several decades have inspired other approaches, including the ethnographic essay, the inquiry-based research essay, and the multigenre paper. All of these alternatives attempt to address the Camp Crescendo problem: How can we turn the research assignment into a meaningful intellectual exercise rather than an empty exercise of "research skills"?

Critics of these alternatives to the conventional research paper complain that they fail to give students practice with argumentative writing, or that they aren't intellectually rigorous, or that they won't help them write traditional papers for other classes. Even some students have their suspicions. If writing a multigenre research paper is actually fun, can it be serious academic work?

What's so important about the book you hold in your hands is that it persuasively and compellingly argues that the multivoiced argument (MVA) does the work that we expect a conventional research paper to do—gives students practice with research skills, helps them write well in other academic situations, and challenges them to think deeply—but it does a great deal more. When writing a multivoiced argument, students are much more likely to understand that argumentative writing is an often nuanced, complex, and most of all, adventurous activity. Argument is not simply lining up ducks but discovering the boundaries of the pond and all the competing perspectives it contains. You only have to listen to Cheryl Johnson and Jayne Moneysmith's students to understand how writing the MVA expands their understanding of argument *and* research. Here's what Jen, one of the students whose project is featured in *Multiple Genres, Multiple Voices* said after writing her MVA: "My experience with argument goes like this: Emotional appeal only takes you so far. Personal experience may be only the basis of an argument, and you must dig much further back to back up your claims. You must string together your claim with character, values, logic, evidence, and emotion."

Jen's sophisticated understanding of the nature of argument is impressive; it includes all the elements of the rhetorical triangle—pathos, logos, and ethos—and it represents a shift in her own thinking, inspired by her MVA on eating disorders. As a young woman who suffered from eating disorders herself, Jen was initially inclined to see her argument in largely emotional terms. That's no surprise. But she later managed to write a multigenre paper that went beyond her own strong feelings about the problem, and as a result was more effective. While Jen's MVA challenged her to employ logos, as well as pathos, in her argument about the causes of eating disorders, this never lessened her engagement with the paper. "This project has me mesmerized," she writes, " . . . I enjoyed every second of it." This is powerful testimony to the impact the MVA pedagogy can have on students' understanding of research, argument, and themselves as active agents who can contribute to public discourse.

The authors of *Multiple Genres, Multiple Voices* anticipate other criticisms leveled at alternatives to the conventional research paper. While it's true that students are currently not likely to be assigned multigenre papers in other classes, Johnson and Moneysmith want to change that paradigm, noting that a multigenre project provides students with a rich rhetorical experience across a broad spectrum of classes from composition and literature to history, psychology, communication, and anthropology. No matter the subject area, students are challenged to choose genres for specific purposes and for specific audiences, and as they struggle to define these, they not only get practice writing for multiple audiences but also gain a much richer understanding of what they're writing about. "Two types of learning took place as I worked on my MVA," wrote Melanie, whose MVA focused on Margaret Atwood's novel *The Handmaid's Tale*. "First of all, there was the knowledge I gained about different issues in America, such as censorship and the religious right. Secondly, and more importantly, I learned to enjoy and respect the idea of the MVA. . . I had some experiences with multigenre writing before, and I didn't consider the projects that I (or my classmates) did to be "academic" enough. . . Once I realized that I had probably done twice as much research for my MVA as I usually do for a traditional paper, I dismissed the idea that the MVA wasn't academic!"

These student testimonials—and the projects students share in *Multiple Genres, Multiple Voices*—convinced me that the authors have indeed made a major new contribution to the discussion about how to teach research-based writing. As promised, they have built on the important pioneering work on multigenre writing by Tom Romano, and extended it in new and exciting ways. The authors, who compare the MVA to a Miles Davis tune—both "improvised and structured"—have brought to the teaching of argument a lively riff that will enliven my classroom. *Multiple Genres, Multiple Voices* will be welcomed, too, by many other writing teachers whose students see argument or research as singing a song they don't have to believe in.

Bruce Ballenger

Chapter One

Multivoiced Argument: A New View

The hardest part about writing a paper is figuring out what to write about. . . . As long as you know the formula (strong intro/strong conclusion, paragraphs in the middle all supporting your thesis) and you, as the writer, make it sound as if you completely believe your argument, then the reader will be convinced, too. (Of course, you don't have to actually believe your argument. You don't even have to care about your argument. You just have to sound like you do.)

Melanie

Melanie's analysis may sound all too familiar. It is the confession of a good writer, one who has learned strategies for writing the successful argumentative essay but approaches it as a game, a matter of filling in the formal requirements without having the slightest personal investment or ethical conviction.

We see writers who are disinterested and disengaged from their texts as a serious problem in our classrooms. We've read through stacks of papers that make the expected moves in academic discourse, but the writers are absent. They cite the opinions of researchers with an occasional *I think* or *in my opinion* added. Such students aren't engaged with their texts.

This was Karen's experience before she wrote her first multivoiced argument:

> I enjoyed research papers because they were easy and basically a no-brainer . . . anyone can write a research paper because somebody already wrote it for you. You grab from everyone else and piece it together and end up with a piece that sounds like a textbook with little or no personal "pizzazz" by the writer. At least this way [writing a multivoiced argument] I can say, yes, I have pieces of information I gathered from others but it is ALL MY PAPER—my personality is in there, and I worked very hard on it.
>
> Karen

Karen's "personal pizzazz" enlivens her argument and assures a more writerly connection to her text. It redefines the kind of argument she presents and reflects our own view of argumentation. In our effort to revamp potentially mind-numbing assignments, we've developed a new approach to argumentative discourse that we call the *Multivoiced Argument* (MVA). We've adapted research on multigenre writing, including the groundbreaking work of Tom Romano, to the rigors of the college classroom, which has traditionally viewed the argumentative essay as the default genre.

We do not advocate abandoning the traditional argumentative essay. We still teach it ourselves, and our students frequently include it as one of their genres in an MVA, or even construct MVAs that consist exclusively of traditional essays written from different points of view. We are aware that there are many definitions of argument and approaches to teaching argument. But this is not a book about the nature of argument. It is a book that presents a method of teaching argument that is flexible and adaptable, and it has helped our students engage their topics. We're aware that the goals of a particular course, the philosophy of a given program, or mandates by a writing director, department chair, or colleagues may make the MVA inappropriate. But in many situations the MVA is not only an appropriate but an outstanding option.

In an MVA, writers create an argument that explores alternative perspectives by using multiple genres written from different points of view. Genres might include a letter, a dialogue, a report, or even a poem—in addition to the traditional essay. Students bolster their argument with research that is reflected within these genres, creating an organic whole, though that "whole" may not be linear. By combining an array of voices with the rigor of scholarship, the MVA offers a fresh and powerful approach to research as argument.

An extended example will demonstrate both what the MVA is and how it differs from traditional argumentative research papers. Let's assume that a student is writing on establishing funding priorities for AIDS research. After extensive reading, she decides that federal funding of AIDS research should be radically increased. In a traditional research-based argument, she would marshal facts to support her point of view. Paraphrasing what the "opposition" thinks, she would try to identify flaws in their reasoning while championing her own point of view. Ideally, all her paragraphs would relate to her main point. This can be a fine way to compose an argument, although it often produces a fatigued and predictable piece of writing.

Were this same student to write a multivoiced argument, she would present her argument differently by including various viewpoints in genres that best express them. Though she would still write the entire argument herself, she would adopt different personas and use a host of perspectives to convince her audience that funding for AIDS research should be dramatically increased. For emotional appeal, she might present diary entries written in the voice of a person with AIDS, or letters this person wrote to a close friend or family member. She might write newsletter articles for a nonprofit organization dedicated to AIDS research, letters to the editor, or fictionalized interviews with AIDS researchers. But her freedom to choose among various genres and perspectives does *not* mean the approach lacks rigor. On the contrary, the author assumes responsibility for meeting both academic and cultural expectations associated with each selected genre. Each reflects the extensive research she has done. By expressing her arguments in varied genres such as testimony before Congress, articles in a professional journal, or a televised debate, the author must think hard about differing viewpoints.

The different types of writing she produces would not result in a haphazard collage or a loosely connected portfolio of work. They would be aimed at a specific audience, which she would define, and they would work together to convey a central, significant point. For example, she could address members at a Congressional hearing, and she could design all her pieces as different types of testimony. This emphasis on audience in the MVA leads students to develop a richer understanding of argumentation. After having taught the MVA in different classes and in different variations, we often hear from students that until they wrote an MVA, they never understood the concept of audience or why it was important in an argument. Writing a multivoiced argument gives students a chance to experience argument as inquiry, a process that leads to exploring, testing, and discussing, rather than focusing on winning a case.

We have found that using multiple voices and genres makes writing researched arguments more engaging. This pedagogy has transformed many students, making them care about their writing, sometimes for the first time in their lives. Melanie, for example (see Appendix A), initially resisted writing an argument without using a traditional "formula." But once she understood what the MVA was all about, she became so immersed in her project that her professor had trouble getting her to stop.

MVA: A Pedagogy Whose Time Has Come

The traditional argumentative model often focuses on finding holes in the "opposition's" argument. While this may be necessary, we are presenting a more varied approach, one that privileges care, connection, cooperation and autonomy and so avoids a risk of traditional argument—silencing the opposition. In emphasizing inquiry as the goal of argument as opposed to "justifying a stance already believed," John T. Gage (1996) observes that "students who believe that they are being taught to argue to prevail over opponents in situations of conflict may believe in consequence that this end justifies any rhetorical practice that leads to winning over or silencing another" (5). To encourage more cooperation and less attention on finding an opponent's weak spot, we redefine *debate* as *dialogue*. But we are aware that keeping the peace does not necessarily mean avoiding conflict.

We are not alone in calling for changes in how to view argument. For example, Catherine E. Lamb (1996) in "Feminist Responses to Argument" states that "techniques of mediation and negotiation provide concrete ways to resolve conflict when the goal is no longer winning but finding a solution in a fair way" (261). The MVA effectively frames such arguments because writers can explore several solutions without favoring one over the other. Instead, writers present substantial information from different perspectives so that the readers can judge which solution best meets their needs. Perhaps the writers will delay the thesis until the end and argue for one solution over the other, but only after they have thoroughly presented a range of solutions to the problem.

Paul Heilker (1996) has argued that our allegiance to the thesis/support model is "developmentally, epistemologically, and ideologically inadequate" (7). Students who choose this "default drive for expository writing" (2) often compose simplistic and safe thesis statements instead of comprehensive and subtle ones. Choosing a simple thesis can make students adopt a voice that ignores or glosses over personal or multivocal perspectives their topics embrace. We have even had students ask us if it is OK to ignore research that does not support their thesis. MVA writers learn how to win over their readers, not by presenting a crisp thesis and lining up reasons and support, like soldiers standing at attention, but by creating a rich text that respects the complexity of a topic. Likewise, readers of an MVA feel not acted on or won over but challenged to work through an issue or problem.

We want our students to *explore* their emerging positions rather than move too quickly to stating a position and supporting it. Such an approach to argument reflects how Pamela Annas and Deborah Tenney (1996) see their students arguing effectively in their classrooms:

> This approach invites students to ground argument in personal experience and belief, to be inclusive of and receptive to alternative viewpoints, to steer a middle way between silence and the assumption of expertise, to be self-reflective and honest about their own assumptions, to keep in mind the material conditions out of which opinions arise and in which they are heard, and to consider their audience as perhaps coworkers toward truth rather than as opponents, dupes, or a row of *tabulae rasae*." (135)

Our students experiment with several approaches to argument and learn that how writers present their claims not only influences the audience's response but also shapes the writers' text.

In "Broadening the Repertoire: Alternatives to the Argumentative Edge," Barry M. Kroll (2000) describes three such approaches—conciliatory, integrative, and deliberative. These approaches resist the agonistic approach to argument and explore different ways for the writer to show that he understands opposing views, can mediate disputes, and discover solutions that will work. The tension in such arguments is related less to who is winning and more to what's at stake and why. We've found that using multiple genres and voices in such arguments has a profound influence on readers and reshapes the rhetorical identity of the writers.

Elisabeth Leonard's (1997) question, "How can I give my students the skills in reading and writing they will need in the academy without denying them the pleasure of becoming an Author?" highlights the importance of experimenting (222). Her answer is to broaden the range of texts in academic discourse and make room for what she calls "fragmented or ruptured" writing (225). Lillian Bridwell-Bowles (1992) suggests that students should write in genres that stretch the boundaries of academic essays. She favors a "diverse discourse" in which alternative writing is placed alongside formal academic arguments (350). Others have taken up Bridwell-Bowles' call. In the past few years, there has been renewed interest in "alt/dis" and in variations of multigenre and multivocal writing. (See, for example, Freedman and Medway 1994; Bishop 1997; Bishop and Ostrom 1997; Romano 1995, 2000, 2004; Davis and Shadle 2000; Allen 2001; Starkey 2001; Schroeder, Fox, and Bizzell 2002.)

We urge instructors to push the boundaries by having students engage multiple genres, "not as 'special' events, things done after the basics" (Bishop 1997, 16) but as significant parts of the curricula. Like Bishop, we don't see this as an either/or issue but as a both/and issue. In Bishop's words, we're "putting the traditional and experimental in dialogue so that we learn about convention making and breaking, who is doing what, in what manner, and why" (13).

In an MVA, the writer takes on different roles but leaves explicit connections that help readers navigate through the sea of voices. The authority of a text rests on two things: engaged readers and conscious writers. The bottom line: constructing an MVA is not like a war but a dance of contrasting yet connected voices.

Practicalities: Fitting the MVA into Our Current Curriculum

The two most common questions people ask us about the MVA are closely related: (1) Can I still meet departmental and university standards when teaching the MVA? and (2) Will the MVA help prepare my students for writing in other classes, such as philosophy, anthropology, or biology? Our answer to both questions is a resounding "yes!"

Though the specific standards that teachers need to meet vary from university to university, we believe that the MVA helps students achieve the core goals shared by the majority of our profession. For example, the standards adopted by the Council of Writing Program Administrators (WPA)—a group composed of administrators from a wide range of programs and institutions—can all be met through teaching the MVA. The "WPA Outcomes Statement for First-Year Composition," adopted in the year 2000, identifies four categories of student achievement, which bear a striking similarity to the aims of the MVA. The "Rhetorical Knowledge" category is especially significant, as this excerpt from the standards shows:

By the end of first year composition, students should be able to:

- Focus on a purpose
- Respond to the needs of different audiences
- Respond appropriately to different kinds of rhetorical situations
- Use conventions of format and structure appropriate to the rhetorical situation
- Adopt appropriate voice, tone, and level of formality
- Understand how genres shape reading and writing
- Write in several genres

In an MVA students write—and think—in different perspectives. Doing so gives them insight into responding to the needs of different audiences, responding to different rhetorical situations, using conventions of format and structure appropriate to the rhetorical situation, and adopting appropriate voice, tone, and level of formality—all identified as desired outcomes by the WPA. Particularly important to our discussion are the guidelines on genre: "Understand how genres shape reading and writing," and "Write in several genres." Assigning essays exclusively limits students' opportunities to develop the range of skills they need. Writing only argumentative essays won't teach students to write in different genres, just as reading financial reports won't teach them to read poetry.

An instructor teaching in a given program may have to fulfill requirements that are quite different from the WPA standards but striving to develop students' critical thinking skills is a pervasive goal throughout higher education. The MVA excels in developing critical thinking skills. Any writing or literature course that stresses critical thinking skills can assign an MVA, even as a major portion of the grade. Multivocal writing requires a more self-reflective and purposeful approach than the traditional essay. Writers must think about several rhetorical requirements: the needs of their audience; the exact language to use; the types of research they need and how to use them; and writing strategies that best suit their purposes. Overall, the MVA makes students better equipped to deal with questions to which there is no easy or readily discernible answer. This kind of knowledge helps students succeed not only in the university but also in their careers.

We also believe that writing the MVA better prepares students for writing in other university courses. When we teach upper-level writing or literature courses—any course beyond first-year composition—we find that the most successful students are those who have the most highly developed critical thinking skills and the widest range of writing skills. These students have become self-aware about the processes of writing and constructing an argument.

Claims that alternative writing does not prepare students for other classes overlook one vital point: student writing in many majors is not confined to writing traditional research essays. In fact, many experts believe that students need to write in a variety of genres throughout the curriculum. For example, Art Young (2003), who helped develop the writing-across-the-curriculum programs at Michigan Technological University and Clemson University, advocates the use of poetry writing in many disciplines. He has found that writing a poem "provides a way into disciplinary discussions in which the writers' own poetic language engages, recasts, and critiques disciplinary knowledge without having to conform to the conventions of what to them is often an alien discourse" or a "formula" they too willingly "mimic" (475). Such genre experiments with poetry deepen students' understanding.

In addition, the writing that students will do after graduation is highly varied. Lawyers write persuasive briefs even when the facts and the law are not favorable. Marketing executives write ads to appeal to various emotions. This is why so many majors now require a course beyond first-year composition devoted to writing in the discipline. It is impossible to expose students to every type of document they will write in the future, nor should we try. What we should do is expose them to a wide range of genres and techniques that have wide applicability and that hone their critical thinking skills. We believe that writing in multiple voices and genres makes it more likely that students will be able to meet writing challenges in other courses and in their chosen professions. Ultimately, the rationale for teaching the MVA boils down to common sense: students learn more because they write more than one type of document and must engage in more varied intellectual activities.

Transforming Writers Through the MVA

When asked to compare her writing of arguments before and after her MVA on eating disorders, student-writer Liz drew a picture of herself as a donkey that refused to budge for her master. A second frame showed the same donkey, chewing on grass, listening to the conversation of her companion. On the back of this picture, Liz wrote:

> I started out set in my opinion, armed with personal experiences and full of emotion. However, the more I read, and the more information I got my hands on, the more I began to question my prior ideas. I saw that perhaps there were other factors behind eating disorders than simply the media and fashion industry. The biological studies opened my eyes and forced me to stretch my writing to include these findings. Throughout the semester, I juggled back and forth between the two, trying to decipher which one I believe in more. . . . Amongst all of the deliberations and questioning, [I realized] I didn't have to decide which side I wanted to be on, I could be on both. I concluded that there is no way to lift the blame completely from the media, but no way could I discount the growing number of studies done on the biological side of this disease. I had compromised. In my first paper I defined my stubbornness as one of my major shortcomings. Looking back, I realize that throughout my suffering, I evolved. I no longer believe there is only one right answer (and that answer has to be mine) or one right way to do things, and this I believe is what I will take with me from the multi-genre assignment for the rest of my days.

Many of our students have reflected similarly on their experiences. We have even had students completely change their point of view once they truly understood the other side of the argument. On the whole, students tell us that constructing a multivoiced argument helped them sift through the various perspectives on a topic and made them consider viewpoints they once dismissed too quickly or ignored. That is reason enough for us to keep assigning multivoiced arguments: students learn to expand and deepen their thinking.

Experimenting with different genres and voices lets students step outside the box, understand other perspectives, and invest themselves in their own writing. One student discovered for the first time what it means to write for an audience and not simply for a grade:

> Not only have I learned fifty times more than I previously knew about depression, I also helped someone else come to terms with their depression and decide to find help through their reading of my MVA . . . . I was informed that it was my MVA and in particular my narrative of my own fight with depression that convinced them to seek help. From that conversation on, I was no longer concerned with my grade on the MVA to tell me whether or not my work might have been effective.
>
> Griffin

Such transformations reveal a profound change, and we could multiply these testimonies beyond our readers' tolerance to hear them. We encourage instructors who try our approach to ask their students to tell their stories about writing multivoiced arguments.

What's Ahead in This Book

In this book we illustrate the MVA by including case studies of two full-length capstone MVAs, that is, MVAs written as final course projects. One MVA is by Jen, Cheryl's student in a writing course, and the other by Melanie, Jayne's student in a literature course. Both are reproduced in Appendix A, along with a sample assignment sheet and "Rationale" form. We have chosen complex projects to illustrate the possibilities the MVA offers. Since our approach to teaching the MVA differs from others in the field, even readers who have done some work with multigenre or multivocal projects will profit from perusing these papers. These same two MVAs are used extensively in Chapter 2, where we discuss the processes of writing an MVA—and include the students' own comments on how they made important decisions about their projects—and in Chapter 4, where we discuss reading, evaluating, and grading MVAs.

Though all chapters fulfill crucial functions, Chapter 2 forms the book's central core. In this chapter we describe the step-by-step process of writing a capstone MVA, from both the teacher's and the student's perspective. We also include specific activities for teaching a capstone MVA in either a writing or a literature course. For teachers who cannot or do not wish to assign a capstone project, Chapter 3 explains how to teach shorter MVAs. In Chapter 4, we show how we read and grade MVAs and give specific criteria for evaluating multivoiced arguments. Following our concluding reflections in Chapter 5, we list and summarize additional sources for teaching multivoiced projects.

Our companion website is an integral part of this book. It includes an extensive collection of materials designed to enhance teaching MVAs, including suggestions for preliminary assignments that set up capstone MVAs, more activities to use in class, shorter capstone projects, assignment sheets, and class handouts. The URL is *www.boytoncook.com/ multiplegenresmultiplevoices*.

Chapter Two

How to Write the Multivoiced Argument

In this chapter we describe the process of writing the MVA in twelve manageable steps. In many instances, we include mini-activities for teachers to use in their classrooms; such scaffolding reduces the anxiety level of both students and instructors. The twelve steps are recursive: writers may need to return to an earlier step to refine and strengthen their papers. Just as important, they are adaptable to individual teaching styles and curricular goals. For example, someone who wants to teach one of the shorter multivocal assignments that we discuss in Chapter 3 may spend very little time on some steps or by-pass them completely.

The twelve steps are as follows:

1. Find an Issue or Problem
2. Choose a Problematical Research Question to Explore
3. Research to Find Answers to Questions
4. Find and Define an Audience
5. Develop the Argument
6. Select Genres to Fit the Audience and Argument
7. Write in Different Genres and Voices
8. Experiment with Different Styles and Voices
9. Develop a Thesis
10. Unify the Genres
11. Document the Research
12. Revise and Edit

As we discuss these steps, we'll include information from our two case studies, Melanie and Jen, to show how these writers created their MVA projects. Consult Appendix A to see their projects and the book's website to examine Gina's shorter capstone project. Though we don't discuss Gina's project in this chapter, she is working through an identical process in her more condensed version.

Step 1: Find an Issue or Problem

As with any argumentative research paper, students first need to find an appropriate issue or problem to explore. To end up with a final MVA that is truly argumentative, students must understand the difference between an issue and a topic. As clear as this distinction may be to instructors, students typically do not initially see the difference or understand why that difference is important. To help them, pose a question like the following: "Would others agree or disagree on how to see, define, or come to terms with your issue or problem?" By choosing a complex issue or problem, students can play different roles and construct texts that address different audiences' needs.

We have found that students better understand the importance of finding an issue or problem when we share the "behind the scenes" processes that authors of sample MVAs went through. For example, Jen's project in Appendix A focuses on eating disorders. She could have written about different types of eating disorders, how common they are, or what treatment options are currently available. When she was at the stage of knowing only that she wanted to write about eating disorders, she didn't yet have an issue. An issue related to an aspect of eating disorders is narrower. In the "Rationale" (available on the book's Web site) she submitted with her completed project in which she explains the choices she made when writing, Jen describes her issue in this way: "I set out to discover the correlation between women's portrayal in the media (particularly advertising) and eating disorders . . . this topic could be problematical because advertisers do not want to be responsible for the snowballing eating disorder syndrome; advertisers want to focus on what sells and succeeds with sales." Health-care professionals, advertising executives, parents, and aspiring models, to name just a few, all have opinions and different perspectives on the relationship between the media and eating disorders. Such conflict is another indicator that Jen has found an issue to address.

From a choice of six novels, Melanie decided to focus on Margaret Atwood's *The Handmaid's Tale*. Disturbed that her classmates were too easily dismissing this novel as unrealistic, Melanie started analyzing the novel's fictional society of Gilead. In her "Rationale" (available on the book's website), she explains that almost immediately she decided "to write a paper that showed the similarities between contemporary American society and the society of Gilead, in order to show that Atwood's fictional society was not as far-fetched as it might appear." Her claim is that our own society reflects the attitudes of the society portrayed in the novel. Not every reader of the novel believes that this connection exists. Not every reader who thinks that Gilead is a believable place and society will think so for the same reasons. These differences give the writer an opportunity to clarify commonalities and resolve some differences.

Students must spend time finding an appropriate issue to write a good MVA. The following activity presents one way to start the process.

The "Dear Author" Letter

Have students write a letter to the author of a text related to the assignment in which they pose questions about the work, focusing on any "controversies" or something that seems problematic. If students have the freedom to choose a topic independent of class readings, they can write a letter to an expert in a field related to their topic. Have students exchange their completed letters with at least one other person in the class, who should give feedback on the ideas the student is discussing ("this part could make a good topic if you narrowed it down") and also try to answer the questions the student has posed. Through this exercise, students often either figure out the answers to their questions themselves or use their initial questions to help develop the problematical question that will guide their research.

In her "Dear Author" letter, Melanie questioned the author about the way she had constructed the society of Gilead, asking her if it was too exaggerated to be effective.

Step 2: Choose a Problematical Research Question to Explore

Once students have found an issue or problem, they must formulate a research question that will guide their research. The students most likely to write provocative and engaging texts are the least content to stay with first impressions. Such writers want to answer their questions in a committed and thorough way and, as readers, we want to hear those answers. Students need to explore their own ideas first and use research as a method for increasing—and supporting—their own understanding of a central issue, not focus their paper primarily on the views of other writers. Just as important, students need to learn that they need not know all the answers when they begin a project. On the contrary, a good research question intrigues writers, motivating them to explore the subject in more thorough and complex ways.

In the "Rationale" for her MVA, Melanie states that her research question became, "What attitudes in America today are similar to those in Atwood's dystopian society?" When Melanie began her project, she did not know enough to answer her question fully and authoritatively, but because she wanted to know the answer, she was willing to investigate censorship and governmental information control, central concerns in the book since only a few citizens of Gilead are permitted to read. Melanie's research question not only helped her locate the most useful types of materials, but also helped her analyze the information she obtained, and even helped her with the actual writing of her paper.

Jen initially had difficulty finding a suitable research issue, as she explains in her "Rationale." Although originally wanting to target only adolescent girls, she ultimately decided to include college-aged women as well. Once she identified both her main research question (Do we need to make a more substantial effort to change how the media shapes our views of the female body?) and her audience (adolescent and college-aged girls), she was ready to think about how best to address this issue.

Step 3: Research to Find Answers to Questions

The advice we give to students doing research for an MVA is similar to the advice we give students beginning a traditional research paper. Our MVA students tell us that they often take our advice much more seriously, however, because they soon realize that they can't just throw in a quotation here and there and call it good, and because the MVA gives them an expanded and more accurate concept of what research really is. Before students begin, we show them completed MVAs and point out the range of ways that writers incorporate research into their genres. Students need to have a sense of the possibilities of the MVA before proceeding.

Our experience shows that students do better when they take control of their research and don't let the "experts" control their thinking. They must follow wherever their research question leads them, including exploring divergent points of view. Students need to use a wide range of sources, even some that they may not typically think of as "research," such as an electronic newsgroup, a radio program, a film, or genres like poetry, plays, and stories. We encourage writers to conduct some field research (interviews, questionnaires, or surveys) in addition to doing standard library research. Often this type of research makes the topic come alive for the student.

Jen did not discover much research directly related to her question; however, she did not change her MVA to "fit" what she found. Rather, because she interacted personally as well as intellectually with her source material by writing extensive dialectical journals for each piece of research she read, she was able to use her research quite effectively to support, clarify, and provide a factual basis for the picture she wanted to paint of eating disorders.

Melanie became intrigued with her project only after she conducted an interview on censorship with a research librarian. When that interview raised compelling issues, Melanie began to pursue her subject vigorously. Melanie also did not confine her research to the first phase of her project; she went back to the research step even after her concept was fairly well developed, whenever she needed to know something to make her project seem persuasive and authentic, as she describes here:

> I used a variety of other research methods to create the various genres in my paper. For example, to write Ms. Johnson's article and assignment sheet, I researched the methods that teachers use to teach *The Handmaid's Tale* in their classrooms. In order to make the church bulletin more realistic, I read bulletins from different churches. I read reviews of *The Handmaid's Tale* and incorporated them into the letter from the librarian to the reverend. I researched the censorship history of *The Handmaid's Tale* and found that it has been contested many times, but I didn't find that it had ever been removed from a classroom or a library, and I based the ending of my paper on this fact. . . . Finally, the emails, while they might appear to just be in the MVA to set the scene or to provide transition, are based on the research that I did while writing the paper, and on my own experiences as a member of a conservative religious community.

Not only did Melanie weave research throughout her process, she also sought material that helped her represent differing views accurately, exploring types of research that never would have occurred to her before. Because students use source material differently in different genres, they often learn far more about research in an MVA than in writing a traditional research paper.

Step 4: Find and Define an Audience

Often students' first response to "Who is your audience for the MVA?" is "anyone who is interested" or "the general reader." But a general audience clouds the focus of an MVA and also makes choosing appropriate genres difficult. Consequently, we require our students to direct their MVAs towards a specific audience. Learning to meet the needs of that audience, while also showcasing alternate views, is one of the major advantages of the MVA approach: it sharpens students' critical analysis skills and gives them important insight into the nature of argument, which in turn prepares them for the challenges of future writing tasks.

Both Jen and Melanie had difficulty deciding on their audience; there were too many choices. By putting themselves in the shoes of potential members of their audience, they were able to understand the assumptions, biases, and principles that might govern an audience's world view. For example, once Jen recognized that her readers might not see the connection between eating disorders and how the media presents the female body, she knew she would have "to paint a clear picture of what damages and risks accompany eating disorders." In her project, she includes pictures of emaciated models and diary entries from an anorexic to demonstrate the tie between ads and self-concept.

Melanie knew most of her classmates thought *The Handmaid's Tale* had no relationship to their own society, and she paid attention to what they said. After a classmate told Melanie that her father described *The Handmaid's Tale* as "nothing but intellectually weak propaganda," Melanie knew that this father had to be a member of her audience. She also knew that she would have to convince him that "our current society is similar to, or could develop into, a society like Gilead."

Both Jen's and Melanie's comments show how a clear sense of audience can help writers refine their purpose and design their argument. The following activity can help students accomplish this goal:

Class Pass

Have each student write down her research question at the top of a sheet of paper and briefly describe her audience in a paragraph. Then, have all students pass their sheet of paper to the left, so that they get another person's research question and audience description. The students' task is to answer that question in one to three sentences, from the point of view of someone they know this issue or problem affects— preferably, one of the members of the writer's defined audience. At the end of their response, they should identify the role they played. Then, they pass the sheet of paper to the left again, and respond to another student's question, and so on. Each time they get someone else's question, they must read everyone else's reaction before they add their own, and they must try to come up with a different angle, add another layer to what someone else has said, or puzzle over the meaning of words or what the implications are for certain positions. By the time students get their own question back, they'll have a composite of answers representing different members of their audience.

The responses to their questions often surprise students. Through this exercise they can begin to see the assumptions and biases that shape people's thinking, which motivates them to return to their research and find ways to understand different positions more fully.

Step 5: Develop the Argument

The success of an MVA often depends on how its argument gets developed, especially in literature classes where little time is spent teaching argumentation. If students have defined their audience well and done the research needed to meet its needs, they should have the tools required to construct a solid argument. Individual pieces or genres may present a direct and distinct argument, but since the entire MVA must be read before readers can discern the writer's overall point, the writer must plan carefully to ensure that the intended perspective is achieved.

To help students build a strong project, we think it makes sense to show them different ways to construct an argument, including the traditional thesis-driven approach. For example, knowing that the audience might be opposed to their views, writers might choose first to summarize their opposition's argument before clarifying the major claim. Or they might explore values and ideas, or various solutions before discussing a specific proposal. These kinds of moves must demonstrate good connection to and understanding of the audience.

Using the Toulmin schemata, for example, can help students construct their arguments before they worry about choosing genres. Jen, for example, constructed a full Toulmin chart before she worried about selecting her genres. (See the book's website for her chart.) It is also useful to model appeals to logos, pathos, and ethos and to focus on defining controversial terms and making key analogies.

Melanie did not construct a Toulmin chart, but she thought carefully about the assumptions and viewpoints of people on both sides of the censorship question. Even in literature classes where not much time is devoted to teaching writing, students who explicitly map out the basic tenets of their arguments will be richly rewarded, a goal the following assignment achieves:

Dialogue for Refining and Developing Your Argument

To help students explore different facets of their argument, have them write a dialogue between two "experts" in the field, or between two characters from a literary work. The first expert or character should describe the student's idea as succinctly and clearly as possible from his or her point of view and in language the expert/character would be likely to use. Once the basic idea has been articulated, the other expert/character should write back, refuting the position the first person has taken. The first expert/character then writes a rebuttal to what the second character wrote, and so on, back and forth, until several good points have been made on both sides. Then ask students to invite a third voice to enter the discussion, one that questions both sides and might even develop a third "take" on the issue. This third voice can bring in issues that students would sometimes rather not think about because they find it easier to think of things as black-and-white. It is a good way, though, to get students to think deeply about their topics and to develop their argument from all angles.

Step 6: Select Genres to Fit the Audience and Argument

Initially students may be confused or puzzled by the term "multi-genre." It's important that they understand that *genre* in its simplest form refers to *types of writing* that adhere to varying conventions of style, form, and structure, while setting up differing expectations on the part of the reader. Students need to become aware that they experience a variety of genres every day: a conversation with a roommate, a song on the radio, email messages, a quiz, a lecture, a grocery list, drafts of essays in a writing group, or one of their own term papers. Living with multiple genres is the norm, and, therefore, learning to write them enhances their lives in school and beyond.

For the MVA, students need to select genres that further their argument and meet the needs of their intended audience. The genre charts depicted in Figure 2-1 categorize commonly used genres in four groups. Group one includes genres that may be considered more "academic," including what some regard as "English-major-type genres," such as critical essays and book reviews. Group two includes public genres such as letters, memos, and brochures. Group three lists more "creative" genres, such as poems, stories, and scenes from plays. Group four contains genres that are visual, such as graphs, cartoons, and other types of illustrations. Usually the best MVAs draw on some genres from each group, but the number and types will vary.

Categorizing genres in this way helps students understand how different types of writing have different conventions and create different expectations for the reader. It is also a good way to guide students so that they develop a broad repertoire of writing abilities, including those identified by departmental and university guidelines. For example, instructors

Figure 2-1
Genre Charts

Group One: Academic Genres		
News articles	Book/film reviews	Classical argumentative essays
Biographical or autobiographical portraits	Your own interview assignment	One or more of your response papers
Case studies	Sermons	Proposals
Editorials	Critical essays	Commentaries
Feature articles	Research reports	Technical reports
Interviews	Theory-based essays	Written debates
Speeches	Mission statements	Point/counterpoints
Group Two: Public Genres		
Police reports	Letters to public officials	Memos
Newsgroup exchanges	Resumes	Job applications
Email exchanges	Letters to the editor	Newsletters or pamphlets
Field notes	Letters to experts	Instructions [how-to guides]
Brochures	Letters of complaint	Lab reports; medical records, doctor's notes
Group Three: Creative Genres		
Poems	Adventures	Newspaper "fillers"
Songs and ballads	Children's stories	Screen plays
Plays, monologues, diary entries, dialogues	Anecdotes	Slide show scripts
Stories, mysteries	Telegrams	Prophesies/predictions

(continued)

Figure 2-1
(continued)

Fantasies, letters to imaginary people/characters/author	TV/radio scripts	Scenes from a play
Riddles	Recipes or menus	Contracts
Epitaphs, obituaries, eulogies, wills	Fables	Lists—grocery, to-do, questions, etc.
Newscasts	Prayers	Quizzes, tests, questionnaires, FAQs
Advice columns	Marriage contracts; divorce contracts; child custody documents	Proverbs
Group Four: Visual Genres		
Graphs/charts	Photos with captions	Collages
Cartoons or comic strips	Illustrations/drawings/engravings/etchings/rubbings	Advertisements, TV commercials
Jokes	Posters	Puzzles
Postcards	Graffiti	Web pages
Bumper stickers	Family tree	Maps
Body art; tattoos	Costumes	Tarot cards; astrological charts

who favor thesis-support arguments could require that an MVA include at least one such essay (as Melanie's does), several genres from Category 1, or only genres from Category 1. Alternatively, instructors can require a variety of genres from multiple groups to teach students a whole range of skills and techniques. No matter the stipulations, students still have some freedom of choice so they can adapt the genres to fit their needs.

These charts are not meant to be exhaustive; instructors can add or delete genres as they see fit. Even though it may seem obvious, we explicitly tell our students that they must write all these pieces *themselves*, not just insert source material written by others. If they choose a cartoon, they must create the cartoon; if they choose a collage, they must create it, all the while integrating into each genre the information they have discovered.

Melanie began her search for appropriate genres by formulating a central concept that would be the driving force of everything that she did in the MVA:

> I first decided that I wanted to tell a story, and planned out a timeline in which the events in the story would happen. I chose my genres because I wanted to allow each of my characters to present their perspective in a written form, but in the form that they would typically write in. For Mollie, the teenager reading *The Handmaid's Tale*, her ideas are expressed through email to a friend and through her poetry, which is a homework assignment. Her teacher, Ms. Johnson, expresses her ideas through an article written for a publication for high school English teachers and through her assignment sheet. Mollie's father, a minister, expresses his views in both letters and in the church bulletin.

Melanie's MVA reads as a gradually unfolding story, with each genre building upon the preceding ones, so that the combined information informs and persuades the readers, creating a unified piece of work.

Jen's project similarly reveals careful attention to purpose and the needs of her audience. To appeal to teachers, Jen chose a genre to match their needs:

> I decided to write a journal article that addressed a real life situation about a student and a teacher. Educators are tools for learning—they possess the control and influence to really make a difference in young people's lives. I addressed this issue by creating a real life scenario where the teacher recognized a change in behavior and took steps appropriate to approaching the problem without overstepping her bounds.

By creating several genres that present different perspectives, Jen compels her audience to face eating disorders in personal and reflective ways. In her "Rationale" she writes:

> Diary entries over a four or five year span from a young girl would mimic the process of an eating disorder—calling attention to the realistic nature of this problem. The purpose of this genre is to create the reality of actually living with an eating problem. The main theme will tie into all other genres to ultimately convince the audience that advertising is a primary instigator of destructive eating behaviors. Journal entries will be a huge appeal to ethos, because this young girl will be talking about her problem in total honesty because, as in the sense that diaries are private, she would be the only one reading them.

After students have completed the research and defined their audience, they are ready to choose genres, using the following kind of activity:

Finding and Testing Genres

Ask students to look at the genre charts and tentatively choose several genres. As an out-of-class activity, have them make a three-columned chart for which they identify their genre choices in column one, their writing personas in column two, and types of research they might include in column three, like this:

GENRES	PERSONAS	RESEARCH
Editorial	Newspaper reporter	Article by Jason Smith
		My interview with Sally

Then have students write a rationale for each genre they have selected, describing why they chose it, and how it will help them meet the needs of their audience and fulfill their purpose. If they have an example of this genre, or you have discussed it in class, they should jot down its formal features; if not, they should go out and find one!

The next class day, students should exchange all their materials with a peer, who should comment on them and help the writer decide whether these are indeed the best genres to choose. Without a structured activity of this sort, students are too likely to choose genres haphazardly. They may, for instance, like the idea of writing diary entries but not think through carefully enough how that genre advances their argument.

Consider facilitating the genre-selection process by collecting examples of as many different ones as possible and giving students the opportunity to examine them in class or in your office.

Step 7: Write in Different Genres and Voices

Students who have written only essays may feel uncomfortable writing new genres. Conducting genre workshops will help them analyze and compose different types of genres. Teachers cannot cover every possible genre that students might include in their projects, of course, but learning to write some of them will help reinforce the basic concepts needed to succeed.

We ask students to bring in copies of editorial cartoons, articles, monologues, dialogues, whatever genre they are interested in. Then, we ask them to do a Genre Analysis before writing in that genre themselves. This way students will identify the features they need to employ. This "thick" reading and writing is essential to exploring a topic. Sometimes students might think, "Well, who doesn't know what a cartoon is?" but requiring them to analyze how both visual and written text in a cartoon shape an argument gives them more to draw on when constructing their own cartoon. These sample genres could be kept in the students' research notebooks. In our classes, a typical sequence for genre-writing days looks like this: peer-feedback on a student draft of a genre, mini-workshop on a new genre (models provided and hands-on workshop follows), and in-class reading aloud or sharing of writing in small groups. In addition, we discuss how to integrate sources into these genres. Outside of class, students are writing their genres while often still conducting research.

In literature classes, we have less time to spend on these activities and usually need to develop additional classroom strategies to give students adequate practice. We might spend 10 or 15 minutes at the beginning or end of class and ask students to write a journal entry in the voice of a particular character. This way students are practicing genre-writing as they are coming to understand a particular work.

The following exercise gives students quick practice writing in different genres and lets them see how the genre impacts the message.

Pick a Genre, Any Genre

Divide the class into groups, and have each one draw a slip of paper from a hat, on which you have written the name of a genre (e.g., poem, letter to the editor, diary entry). Then distribute another handout that contains a general prompt to which each person should respond using the genre chosen for that group. It also helps to include on the handout a quick list of criteria that each genre should fulfill. For example, a literature class studying *The Awakening* might receive a prompt saying, "Using the genre your group has chosen, express shock, horror, and/or moral outrage at Edna's suicide, written from the point of view of a character in the novel." One group might write a diary entry, another a poem, yet another a letter to a friend. A writing class might also be asked to respond to an assigned reading or to write on a specific issue. Have group members exchange drafts and comment not only on how well the draft meets the criteria for the genre, but also on how "authentic" the voice sounds. Ask each group to read one response to the class, so everyone can hear how the same basic idea takes on such a different cast depending on the genre and voice used.

Step 8: Experiment with Different Styles and Voices

In addition to practice in writing different genres, students need practice learning to compose in different styles and voices. Devising separate workshops on style will help students further revise their genres. The kinds of stylistic choices a writer makes in an MVA depend on the purpose, audience, writer, and genre. For example, the informal, personal style of Jen's journal entries, written from the vantage point of a young girl with an eating disorder, differ markedly from the professional, no-nonsense article she wrote to convey the seriousness of this condition. Melanie's project, too, uses a wide range of styles, ranging from the informal, chatty email messages from the young teenager Mollie, to the professional, academic prose of Ms. Johnson's article in *The English Journal*, to the folksy, often humorous pieces in the local paper. In her "Rationale," Melanie mentions the care she took in trying to make each voice sound "authentic." Even if students ultimately decide not to use genres produced during in-class workshops, this type of practice will increase their sensitivity to style and improve all their written products.

Step 9: Develop a Thesis

Unlike a traditional research paper, the MVA probably won't begin with an introductory paragraph ending with a thesis. In fact, the thesis may not be explicitly stated at all, though by the time readers finish the text, they should have a clear understanding of the writer's purpose. For example, Jen's thesis—that media images of women are damaging because they encourage eating disorders, poor self-esteem, and the desire to attain an unrealistic body-type rather than intellectual and emotional development—rings clear. Different parts of her MVA illustrate this idea in different ways, ranging from expert viewpoints to a print ad that illustrates the problems caused by the media.

In contrast, Melanie set out to include opposing points of view in her MVA, believing that readers will eventually see which side of the argument she favors. Her MVA tells the story of a parent seeking to ban *The Handmaid's Tale* from the school library. His failure underscores her argument.

Though students sometimes arrive at their thesis earlier in the process, we want to emphasize that students come to understand their thesis as the project evolves. Students who have difficulty formulating their thesis can revisit their problematical research question. What answers to their question does their research suggest? If they are unsure about what they want their readers to understand, students need to return to their audience description to develop a better sense of the audience's biases and assumptions.

Step 10: Unify the Genres

Students often worry needlessly about unity. If they've spent quality time developing a good argument, defining their audience, and selecting appropriate genres, they should not have serious problems.

In a text that uses various voices and genres, students need to make sure that readers can follow a trail. An MVA is not aimless or arbitrary. Unlike a traditional essay, the MVA won't often use transitional words (*as you can see, in contrast, similarly,* etc.) between sections, but writers must still find a way to make their paper cohesive, or readers won't grasp their argument.

Jen, for example, ended up with an excellent project, but initially she was not sure the parts would fit together. Her decision "to create Disordered Media, Inc., an organization dedicated to helping improve the images of women gracing the media and ultimately soothe the harmful results they cause," gave her project the focus and coherence it needed. Melanie designed her MVA so that "the reader must piece together the story as it unfolds and determine what the main argument of the MVA is. The genres work together in chronological order to tell a story," with the email messages providing the backbone of the project.

For students who need ideas to help them unify their projects, some of the following strategies might be useful:

- Create an overarching framework that brings the disparate pieces together, such as beginning with a letter, preface, or other device that provides a cover story for the entire project.

   Example: A student who became fascinated with the life of Emily Brontë after reading *Wuthering Heights* wrote a series of diary entries, supposedly by Brontë herself, to reflect the biographical facts she discovered. Her project begins with the letter to a museum curator in which she explains that her late husband had found a previously unknown diary of Brontë's. In the letter she explains the time period and subject matter covered by the diary entries, indicates that they show a direct link between the author's life and poems, and argues for the diary's value. (She even asks the museum curator if he would like to purchase it!).

- Set the scene with a first piece that anchors all the others.

   Example: A project arguing for increased funding for AIDS research is organized as a series of letters between a young man dying of AIDS and his aging parents. The first letter in the series sets up the whole situation. Within the letters are enclosures, such as news articles (which were really short essays the student wrote), poems, extracts of diary entries, etc.

- Design the project around one central writer, whose voice provides unity.

   Example: A project arguing that Native American traditions must be preserved is written in the form of a memoir an elder composes for his grandchildren. Included in the memoir are stories of the tribe's history, customs, and religion, along with myths, interviews, letters, and drawings.

- Begin each section or genre with a short note that explains its content and how it relates to the whole.

Example: For each section of a project on Sara Winnemuca, author of *Life among the Piutes,* the student writes a few lines that set the scene and provide context.

- Alternate opposing views.

Example: A project on *Pride and Prejudice* presents a series of essays that give alternating views about one of the major characters, Mr. Darcy.

- Create a hypertext project around one central essay, which contains multiple links to other views. In more sophisticated projects, the MVA can bring in the reader at different points and with varying results, depending on how the text is navigated.

Example: A hypertext project about the slave trade in the Caribbean in the eighteenth century begins with a traditional essay that gives the basic facts of the slave trade but is linked to many sources of information.

- Use formatting and visual elements to create unity.

Example: We have had many students set up their project as a magazine or newsletter, using the publication's design to create unity.

Whatever choice they make, students will discover that choosing a structure has a powerful impact on their readers. To give them practice, try the following activity:

Reconstructing an MVA

Divide the class into groups, and give each one a large manila envelope in which you have put all of the "pieces" of a finished MVA that you have taken apart and from which you have removed page numbers and anything thing else that may show the intended order. Have students look at all the pieces and then discuss what clues they find to its interior unity. Each group should come up with a proposed order of the pieces, a rationale for that order, and a description of anything that they would add to enhance unity; for example, an opening piece that pulls it all together. Have groups report back to the class. Finally, show them how the original MVA is constructed and share the writer's comments on why it is organized this way. Whether or not students guess correctly how the original is constructed, they will have gained valuable insight into the concept of unity.

Step 11: Document the Research

Our students use MLA style to document their sources, but, depending on the genres chosen, they may do the citations differently than in a standard research paper. Here are some guidelines:

- *For sections of traditional essay:* have students use standard parenthetical citations, with the author's last name and page number in parentheses, which then correlate with a "Works Cited" page.

  Example: "Genre writing is a great idea" (Bishop 12).

- *For genres other than the essay:* have students use notes to indicate their sources so their creative work looks more authentic. Insert a footnote number at the end of the sentence that needs documenting, and then give the necessary note either at the bottom of the page or with all the notes at the end.

  - *Use notes to indicate the source of a direct quotation, or summarized or paraphrased material*: the note should direct readers to the "Works Cited" page by giving the author's last name and page number.

  - *Use notes to tell readers what research a creative section is based on*: have students give the explanation and direct the readers to the "Works Cited" page.

    - *Example:* I wrote this diary entry based on the impression I got of the author from reading Miller, Chaps. 2 and 3.

Sometimes students adapt our guidelines and create a modified system of their own. Melanie resisted using even small superscript numbers in her text; she felt that they were artificial. Instead, she included a "References" sheet at the end of her MVA, in which she explained her choice of sources. One of Cheryl's literature students used a similar approach, noting each source and how he used it on the "Notes" page. The reader could see firsthand how the writer understood the information. No matter what system they use, students need to learn the importance of careful and correct attribution.

To give students information on the physical format for documenting their research and on the content of their citations, try the next activity.

Documenting Sources

Make overheads of the "Notes" page and the "Works Cited" page of a strong MVA to showcase expectations for documentation. Draw the class's attention to how a writer uses a superscript, then show how the footnote corresponds, and, finally, show how the source is fully notated on the "Works Cited" page. Be prepared to explain how to make superscripts, or even prepare a handout if students don't know. To give them practice, show them an excerpt from an MVA that clearly needs some kind of documentation, and have them discuss how they might do it. Give them practice doing "Works Cited" entries by having them write a few entries that would correctly correspond to a few of the notes.

In our experience, students usually do not choose standard MLA format for this project, knowing that real letters to the editor don't use that style and that it would make their project seem phony. Instead, they may prefer the superscript method or the type of in-depth explanations that Melanie used.

Step 12: Revise and Edit

Because MVA writers must integrate divergent styles and genres into a unified whole, they often need to revise and edit more thoroughly than writers of traditional research papers do. As a result, students typically emerge from the MVA experience with a greater appreciation of the importance of these steps. Providing a structured approach to revision helps.

We often workshop one or two students' complete drafts in class, using the Critique Guidelines in Chapter 4. Students may also profit from receiving a list of questions and solutions to help them further critique their own texts, such as the following:

- For each genre, ask yourself these questions: Does it develop my thesis or is it unnecessary? Does it explain something that's key to understanding what I'm trying to say? Does it illustrate a key concept? Does it raise a question that I must explore? Does it illustrate reasons and evidence to support my major claim? Be willing to throw out what's not working and to add new material to fill in the gaps.

- If the connections between genres confuse your readers and you, what might help to weave a tighter fabric? Revisit the different strategies to achieve unity and try out a new scheme on a reader.

- How might you become more independent of your sources so they don't dominate your text? How might you examine facts in your genres and not simply drop them from the sky, hoping your reader will be impressed?

- How might you address further the concerns of your audience? How might you show that you see numerous ways to approach your issue, not just a single view?

We try to make revising a playful process. Too often students approach re-writing like going in for a root canal or picking lint off a sweater. Successful MVA projects demand deep revision, not a mere clean-up of surface errors. Sentence-level editing is particularly important for genres with which students are unfamiliar, especially when they are writing in the "voice" of someone whose ideas differ from their own, but they must go beyond that. The following two activities assist students in first examining their project globally and then at the sentence level.

What Color is Your MVA?

Bring in old magazines, construction paper, glue sticks, and other decorative items (ask students to bring some, too). Have students choose a color of construction paper that they think reflects the mood or tone of their MVA. On the back of the paper, they should list their research question, their thesis, and their audience. Then they should turn over the paper and begin assembling a collage comprised of both pictures and words that they believe reflects the essence of what they are trying to convey in the MVA. When they finish, have them write a "Rationale" for their collage in which they explain why they chose the materials included in the collage and how the collage as a whole reflects the spirit of their MVA. Have at least one other person look at the collage and the "Rationale," and then skim the MVA. How effective is the collage? This project helps students think about their nearly finished projects in a fresh and original way.

Policework: Editing the Multivocal Argument

Students should form a large circle and pass a copy of their own drafts to the left. Ask the class to count off by fives (assuming five police teams). For each number, one through five, assign a specific task, one that you have outlined on a handout. For example, ask members of the Concise Police Team to eliminate redundancies, cut empty or inflated phrases, etc. Other "police teams" might include Active Voice, Comma Splices and Run-ons, etc. Consider providing colored pens, one color for each team. Have each student look for the things specified for his or her team in the first three pages of a peer's draft and correct them, and when finished, pass the draft to the next person, and so on, until each paper has been reviewed by a member of each team.

> Asking students to focus on just one problem in each draft helps both writer and reader. Once their texts are returned, students can analyze the suggestions of their peers and apply them to the rest of their draft. Though we present this activity as fun, the word "police" suggests serious work to students and gives them a sense of authority.

We have found that students need to work through all twelve steps to write a high-quality MVA. Although we do not always have the class time to instruct them on every single step, we try to give them assignments that teach important skills and strategies. For example, we might ask students to write a prospectus in which they indicate their research question, the basic framework of their argument, their sources, and what genres they might use. With students practicing different genres, voices, and styles long before we start a capstone MVA in journal entries or short papers, they usually already feel comfortable with the basic concepts. Finally, our students often use papers they have written previously in the semester as part of their MVA or write papers on the same topic to deepen their perspective. See the book's Web site for some sample preliminary assignments you might use to set up the MVA. In the next chapter, we give suggestions for teaching shorter MVAs.

Chapter Three

Shorter Multivoiced Assignments

Since teachers do not always have time to assign a full-length capstone multivoiced argument, we want to describe shorter versions that still allow students to gain expertise in voice and genre. Many of the steps and exercises in Chapter 2 can be used for these assignments.

In the following pages, we present six different assignments that could be easily adapted for a variety of literature and writing classes. The first one, the paired genre project, is a universal assignment that can help students reap many of the benefits of multivocal writing and is useful as an introduction to this kind of pedagogy. The remaining five assignments offer various possibilities that will work in different teaching environments.

The Paired Genre Project

Although it takes less time to complete, the paired genre assignment allows students to practice writing arguments from different perspectives, including the intended audience's viewpoint. We begin by asking students to select two genres that will enable them to persuade an audience to accept their position or solution. The first genre in each pair should express the writer's main stance, demonstrating to his or her chosen audience why this stance is the most reasonable. Students might compose a traditional thesis-driven essay, or newspaper editorial, etc. The second genre explores responses to the first position, airing the voices of both opponents and supporters and leaving readers with hard choices. The paired genres push both writers and readers toward a more complex understanding of the subject.

For example, one of our writing students chose as his first genre an editorial in which he argued that wolves should be reintroduced into Idaho's wilderness areas. In his two letters to the editor, he showcased the contrasting views of a farmer and a backpacker. For a project on Mary Shelley's *Frankenstein* in a literature class, a student wrote a critical essay on the character, Clerval, in which she summarized key critical perspectives before presenting her own view of the role he plays as a double for Victor. For her second genre, she wrote a letter from Clerval who voiced his unhappiness at the way critics have portrayed him.

Here are some genre pairs that work well together:

- critical essay and letters of response (or any of the second genres below)
- editorial and two letters to the editor
- news or feature article and two letters to the editor
- brochure and reactions (in the form of two letters, a written debate, or discussion at a board meeting or public forum)
- exterior monologue and ensuing debate at a forum or public meeting
- letter exchange between experts/public officials and members of the audience (one main letter plus two letters of response)
- memo and a discussion/debate at a meeting or forum
- a play and a review of the play (the review would represent the views of the audience)
- a TV or radio script and a review (the review would represent the views of the audience)
- a cartoon sequence and a review (the review would represent the views of the audience)

Using the process we outline in Chapter 2, teachers can pick and choose which steps and exercises to assign, and how many secondary sources to require.

Because we feel we need to teach students how to write a critical essay in a literature class, we often limit the choices to a required critical essay and then offer a wide choice of creative second genres. In class, we discuss the critical essay and show how we, as writers, might respond to it in various genres. For writing classes, providing written copies of the genres in the above list helps students analyze the possibilities, or they can bring in examples of each pair and discuss them in small groups. Samples could be posted around the classroom, and a speaker from each small group could summarize their group's observations on the audience, purpose, and argument for each.

Analyzing genre, audience, and argument will help students practice critical thinking skills before they select the pair they want to develop. In a literature class, we don't teach the appeals to logos, pathos, and ethos in quite the same way but prefer to focus on the ways argument is developed in critical contexts.

To illustrate the possibilities for this assignment, a sample paired genre exercise is included on the book's website *www.boyntoncook.com/ multiplegenresmultiplevoices.*

Linking Drama or Film to Multigenre Argument

Writing a play can teach students how to explore multiple viewpoints while influencing an audience's perspective. Some of our students view films and plays as entertainment and resist analyzing them *as argument.* However, they can be taught the persuasive appeal of such genres, thus learning that many arguments are won or lost through dialogue. How the characters engage in that dialogue not only determines the outcome of crucial issues, problems, and events but also defines how we see ourselves in this world and how we imagine others see us.

After choosing an issue and researching it, students are asked to construct a play that explores the topic. For example, a literature student explored the husband's relationship to his wife in Charlotte Gilman's *The Yellow Wallpaper* by reading background material on nineteenth century marriages, locating information on Gilman's marriage, investigating health care issues, and interviewing a professor on campus who has done research on Gilman. This student showed the husband in a favorable light, arguing that he was a product of his culture.

A composition student used her service-learning experience as a substitute for the interviews (a choice we offer and encourage). Focusing on depression among the elderly, she returned to the nursing home where she had volunteered, became part of the fabric there, and used those interactions, observations, and discussions as sources for creating multiple perspectives in her play. The journal entries we require for a service-learning component in our persuasive writing classes helped this writer reconstruct the voices of the nursing home residents.

As a way to model this process, students could study a work like Moises Kaufman's *Laramie Project,* which centers on the 1998 murder of University of Wyoming student Matthew Shepard. Kaufman and others conducted over 200 interviews of residents in Laramie, condensed them and, along with journal excerpts from the theatre group's members and court records, created a three-act play that focuses on gay rights. Based on their study of a play and possible viewing of the play on stage or on film, students can write a review that analyzes how the work develops its argument, relates to the audience, deploys specific presentational strategies, etc.

If there's not enough time to assign such a review as a preliminary step to creating a play, consider devising a role-playing activity such as the following:

Acting Scenarios

Ask students to participate in a public gathering, one that is focused on a key issue or problem that you phrase in a question (e.g., "Should high schools permit gay-straight alliance clubs?"). This could be a school board meeting or a forum for which you write a paragraph scenario, summarizing why this meeting has been called. Each student must draw a slip of paper from a hat. On each slip, the teacher identifies the community member the student will need to role-play and writes a short character sketch of this person. If you want to give your students a chance to prepare, they could draw their roles ahead of time. Appointing one student to emcee and certain members to prepare statements of their positions will help structure the proceedings. There should be ample time for discussion after these short speeches. This activity helps students realize that writing a play, based on an issue or problem, is not outside their experience.

This activity takes a full class period, one that might be followed up with a written summary of that day's proceedings and discoveries.

A Self-Portrait

Writing a multigenre self-portrait enables students to explore their own layered identities by examining various facets of themselves, including the personas they think the world sees. In this respect, the genres they choose should convey a specific claim about who they are, not as a haphazard collage of impressions but as an argument for defining themselves in a certain way. Whether students write an autobiography, a poem, a dialogue of contending voices, a diary entry from someone else's point of view, a scene from a play in which others talk about them—every genre must convey a specific claim about who they are. Each answers this central question: Who *is* that reflected image in the mirror?

For a writing class, students might read excerpts from Daniel Halpern's *Who's Writing This?* which shows how writers use various genres and perspectives to reflect who they are. Halpern asked about fifty authors to write a self-portrait of themselves as writers and to accompany each self-portrait with a drawing or depiction of themselves. We asked our students to apply what they observed in Halpern's text to explore personality traits that form their own *essential* identity.

For a literature class, we adapted this assignment for a unit on autobiographies. Students had just read Rousseau's *Confessions*. They struggled with the persona projected by Rousseau, an apparently self-absorbed man who didn't feel others had treated him fairly. To explore how different views of the same incident significantly shape how we see someone (such as the incident of the stolen comb for Rousseau), we asked students to explore their own lives and focus on key incidents that might be variously interpreted. Their multifaceted self-portrait gave them a fresh understanding of Rousseau's claims about his life and how his culture and family shaped his identity. This kind of assignment works well in any class reading biographies, autobiographies, or memoirs.

To encourage our students to see the complexity of their own identities and how others might interpret them, we ask them to complete the following reflection on themselves.

Exposing the Underbelly

1. Make two lists: one labeled, "I'm not" and the other labeled, "But I am." Write down all the ways you think the world sees you in the first column and how you see yourself in the second column.

2. List the things you keep in your closets, drawers, cars, or even the refrigerator.

3. Empty the contents of your backpack, purse, or wallet on your desk and describe them. Then, write down any reflections you have on what these activities reveal about yourself. In pairs, share your lists, and for #3, record your observations on what your partner's contents suggests. Comparing notes and lists will help you see how others perceive you and how you see yourself.

The self-portrait assignment has wide applications. It works well in any writing course as a first assignment and in literature classes where students are reading biographical or autobiographical works, or are reading literature that focuses on the theme of *identity*. Some students will feel shy about writing about themselves, so it is important to create a comfortable atmosphere in the class, one that emphasizes trust and affirmation.

Multigenre Biographies

Unlike the previous assignment, which focuses on the students, this project asks students to create a portrait of another person, enabling them to view their interviewee in a certain way. Students use a variety of genres (poems, news articles, letters, diaries, etc.) and voices (from their interviewee, and from others who know them) to create a complex biographical and multidimensional portrait. Ultimately, the piece should form an *argument*—that is, it should invoke an argument out of biographical experience.

For this assignment, we have several requirements. First, students must complete interviews with two different people: a primary interviewee—the person on whom their project will focus—and a person who knows their interviewee well. Secondly, their major interviewee should be a member of a "community" to which they belong, but differ from them in some significant way. This person might be someone from another culture, race, generation, gender, or walk of life—a puzzle that others want to understand better or someone who genuinely puzzles them.

In addition to conducting two interviews and using that information in their project, they need to read any primary or secondary sources available that will help them learn more about their interviewee (letters or newspaper articles written *about* this person, other written interviews *with* this person, any articles/essays/books written *by* this person). They also need to read information on the issue they identified and topics they know are important to their interviewee.

Their interviews form the basis of a project in which they present the "voices" of their interviewees alongside their own, using multiple genres such as monologues, debates, narrative, poetry, diaries, and letters, as well as sections of traditional essay. Students in our writing classes have explored interesting characters, including a former member of the Hell's Angels and an aunt who died years before the writer was born, but who left a series of revealing letters. Students in our literature classes must interview someone who has a connection with an issue or idea reflected by one of their assigned texts. For example, a student who had trouble identifying with Tita's passion for cooking in *Like Water for Chocolate* interviewed the award-winning chef of a new restaurant because the chef had been quoted as saying that she infused love into her cooking—just as Tita did. When the student arrived at the restaurant, the chef not only answered her many questions but also lent her a scrapbook of newspaper clippings about her, and arranged for her to talk to another chef with whom she had worked for many years. She also gave the student a gift certificate so she could enjoy dinner at the restaurant and experience the chef's unique recipes. In her final project, the student was able to build a very rich verbal portrait of the chef, pulling in a variety of voices, including her own, while making connections to *Like Water for Chocolate*.

Reading Multigenre Biographies

Reading Michael Ondaatje's *The Collected Works of Billy the Kid*, an unconventional biography focusing on the last few years of Billy the Kid's life, enables students to see the possibilities of multigenre work, both as writers and readers. This assignment is helpful to students who are about to write their own multigenre biography, but it can be adapted for a class reading any multigenre or multivocal work—including our sample MVAs.

The purpose of this assignment is to analyze *how* Ondaatje constructs Billy's identity, how and why he used a variety of genres and personas, and how his research on Billy comes through. Because students might resist reading such a text closely, we've devised an activity that gets them inside a text and its writer.

On Reading Ondaatje

To jumpstart a class discussion, use the following questions as prompts for ten-minute writes at the beginning of class or as a possible quiz.

1. How does Ondaatje create characters and from what points of view?
2. How does he transition between personas?
3. What genres does he use and for what purposes?
4. How do these multiple genres work on you?
5. How does Ondaatje, as narrator, enter the text?
6. How does the nonchronological order work on you?
7. How would you describe the language rhythms?
8. How did you react to the sexually explicit parts or the scenes of violence?
9. Are these passages pornographic or areas of concern if you wanted to use this book in a high school classroom?
10. How does Ondaatje create cohesion, or does he?
11. What seems to be Ondaatje's main claim, and how does he support this claim?
12. To what would you compare your way of reading this text? Reading Ondaatje is like . . .
13. As documented research, comment on the author's credibility as a researcher.
14. Imagine this text as something else (a poison, a medication, a member of one of the sexes, a spouse, a kind of weather) and explore its life and implications.

This activity can lead students to write a careful analysis of *how* the different genres and voices work together to form a rich portrait of *the kid,* or it can serve as a preliminary activity for students writing their own multigenre biography. Similar questions can be devised for any multigenre or multivocal work, such as *Fried Green Tomatoes, Like Water for Chocolate, The Blind Assassin,* and any of the sample MVAs in the Appendix or on the book's website *www.boyntoncook.com/ multiplegenresmultiplevoices.*

Layered Intrusions

Students first read Ursula Hegi's *Intrusions,* a novel in which the author frequently interrupts her primary narrative—with thoughts about writing the novel, voices from her own family members, comments from her characters, and even conversations between her real family members and her made-up characters—and then they write their own narrative using some of Hegi's "intruding" techniques. If teachers do not have time to assign the entire novel, they can easily illustrate Hegi's approach by showcasing and discussing a short section of her novel on an overhead. We describe the assignment here focusing on Hegi's novel, but many different novels would work, as we explain below.

In actual life, Hegi is trying to balance the demands of marriage and children with her own need to write, while the protagonist of the novel is feeling similar frustrations. The theme of *Intrusions* is how these expectations create and frustrate *real life*. In addition to the genre of fictional narrative, she uses newspaper accounts, headlines, dialogue, diary entries, photo captions, drawings, index cards, ads, and letters. In this way she creates a rich metadiscourse that challenges us to read differently, and, in effect, we become characters too.

To create such an experimental text, our students must:

1. Create a story or daydream in which they *intrude* and in which their characters, in turn, can *intrude* on them

2. Allow different characters to speak (from the story they create and from the *real* life drama they include)

3. Use a variety of genres (at least three) as part of their main story line or as part of the writers' lives

To get to this point, however, students need to understand the novel, as both readers and writers. As with Ondaatje's *The Collected Works of Billy the Kid,* we ask students to examine *how* Hegi writes. The activity in the previous section, "On Reading Ondaatje," can be adapted to Hegi's text as well.

After students explore and discuss Hegi's writing style, they can practice her rhetorical moves by completing the following activity:

Layering Fiction and Nonfiction

Ask your students to create a story or daydream based on their own life. Develop a list of scenarios for your students to explore and ask them to freewrite on each to see if any will lead them to a "story" that will work with their life. For example, one scenario might be: *You are a student. How might your life as a student intrude on a story or daydream you're trying to create, one that connects to your own life in certain ways?* Point out that Hegi writes a story about Megan, whose expectations don't match her experience. It's not by chance that Megan is also married and has children, like Hegi in actual life. Your students need to find connections between their actual lives and the life they are creating. Hegi, for example, plays with the idea that she's creating these characters quite apart from herself. But her characters argue with her; they say she's making them behave a certain way—that she's transposing real life on to their fictional life. Your students' "stories" or "daydreams" might be a piece of fiction they generate before the readers' eyes, quite self-consciously the way Hegi does. Students need to develop characters, conflict, a problem to work out.

Though this "intruding" assignment is based on Hegi's novel, it can be adapted to many other texts that contain multiple voices and narratives. For example, in his graphic novel/memoir *Maus,* Art Spielgelman reveals his own angst and problems as he wrote the book. He shows himself talking to others about writing it, and sometimes even says that he doesn't know how to write a certain section—and then goes on to present that section. Though a very different work than *Intrusions, Maus* presents many different kinds of intrusions on the central story, so that the work becomes more about writing itself than about his father's life. The assignment could be applied to any novel containing more than one perspective, ranging from Dickens's *Bleak House* to Julie Otsuka's *When the Emperor Was Divine.* The type of "intrusion" can be altered, depending on the accompanying assigned reading, or students can write independently from an assigned text. For example, students could write an essay on a controversial issue in which they periodically "intrude" on their text. They can step out of their persona as essay writer and insert snatches of narrative that give personal comments on the issues they have been describing. In a literary critical essay, a student can intrude by inserting informal journal comments made during her first reading or comments on her writing process. Such "intruding" helps students blend self-reflection and metadiscourse on their own reading and writing processes.

Adapting Assignments to a Multivoiced, Multigenre Framework

As we demonstrate throughout this book, writing from multiple perspectives in multiple genres enables students to engage in complex analysis, to better understand audience, and to be more open to opposing viewpoints. Such writing, however, does not necessitate that an instructor's entire pedagogy be revamped. Students can gain the advantages of this approach even when an instructor makes some fairly small adaptations. For example, in a writing class, instead of asking students to write a standard description of their audience in paragraph form, consider asking them to analyze audience by putting that description in the audience's own words. In a literature class, instead of writing a standard character analysis, have students write diary entries that reveal the character's true self. Virtually any assignment can be "converted" to a multigenre or multivocal one, with good results.

Helping students expand the range of discourse for arguments can also help them discover approaches to their subjects that will be forceful and memorable. As one of our students, Jeremy, explained after completing a shorter multivocal assignment,

> Writing the Self-Portrait paper was like being introduced to an old friend who has, in the last few years, turned into a drunken, dirt-eating, nasty magazine-reading old man. I thought I had rid myself of that guy, but apparently he is attempting to surface in my writing. . . . The paper taught me an important lesson: when you finally decide to kill parts of your old self, make sure they are dead, dead, dead. Otherwise, you end up with a paper that only receives an A-, which is not too bad, but would be better had the drunken man not been around.

Another student, Megan, wrote that "one huge benefit [of this multigenre work] is that we'll remember the content of our papers much more than in classes that require traditional essays." That is reason enough to consider assigning any of the shorter assignments!

Chapter Four

Revising and Evaluating the Multivoiced Argument

Good writing keeps us awake, but too often student prose trudges rather than soars. The MVA is our answer. It has allowed students to find their wings and compose work that is lively, engaging, and compelling. That their projects are also varied and distinctive in form and function, however, poses particular challenges to both students and instructors. We have addressed many of those challenges in previous chapters, but it is now time to turn our attention to two specific difficulties, one of which affects students, the other of which affects instructors. We are speaking, here, of reading and evaluating multi-genre and multivocal texts.

In this chapter, we examine both of these topics. First, we describe how we teach our students about revision by helping them learn how to read an MVA. In particular we have found it important to share with them specific criteria that can be applied to virtually every piece within the MVA. We then describe some hands-on peer review strategies that guide students toward revising from an audience perspective. Finally, we conclude by offering some practical guidelines for grading that have helped us to discover the particular insights and achievements of our students.

Revising Reading Habits

To understand a rich, multivocal text, and thus provide feedback that will help writers revise, readers need to refine their usual reading habits and give the writing a chance to work. Lacking the usual clues (linear structure, clear transitions, classical frame with a self-announced thesis in the introduction), readers should approach an MVA patiently and recursively, letting perspectives comment on each other. Although individual genres may present a specific point of view, the entire project must be read to determine its overall point. Students can best learn how to do this when the entire class works through one or more sample MVAs, with special attention paid to the following features:

1. Purpose: Unlike a classical argument, the thesis or claim typically will not be announced in the first or second paragraph. In fact, the writer may choose to begin with a slogan or ad or a letter and not with an introductory paragraph. The MVA writer, however, is responsible for presenting different views of an issue in a way that ultimately makes clear his or her major claim.

2. Unity: Readers are accustomed to viewing paragraphs like boxcars in a train, linked with clear transitions. If constructed well, MVAs embody logic; students often work hard to give clues so that no one feels stranded or confused. In Chapter 2, we gave several strategies for creating unity and cohesion. Still, the connections are not always direct and immediate, and readers must adjust to a nonlinear presentation.

3. Voice: Readers will hear not one but several voices that comment on each other, like going to a party and talking at length to several friends about the same topic. Thinking back, we remember parts of conversations that grow into an overall impression. Reading several genres in different voices is similarly challenging and invigorating. The text isn't monotone, but multitone, and readers must absorb the thought patterns of the text, rich in research and critical inquiry, letting the argument work on them. In short, finding meaning is reciprocal. True, the MVA writer must satisfy all the criteria in our grading grids, but the readers must actively participate in making meaning.

4. Genres: Readers must move through several different genres in an MVA project. By paying close attention to genre formation and rhetorical decision-making, students learn that each genre must conform to conventions and that all genres are not appropriate for any given situation. Such insights pay great dividends to writers. Students will also benefit from reading a work that uses multiple genres—either a published text (like *The Collected Works of Billy the Kid*) or on the book's website *www.boyntoncook.com/multiplegenresmultiplevoices.* We often share student-authored MVAs, since they have great instructional value.

Peer-Reading of Genres

Writers need several opportunities to test their writing on their classmates. Our students frequently bring one of their genres to class for feedback instead of waiting until the end of the term to workshop their entire draft. This way, students can make improvements as they write, and they are less prone to procrastinate. The following activity can help students rethink their genre choices and build a case for using them. This activity helps students make informed choices based on audience awareness, purpose, and knowledge of each genre's capabilities.

Workshopping Single Genres

On workshop days for single genres, ask students to respond in writing to the following prompts:

- Identify your problematical question for the issue or problem
- Describe your intended audience
- List other genres you'll probably use in your project
- Explain the major claim or point you want to get across in this selected genre

Require students to exchange drafts in pairs. Each student first reads the description of the intended audience for the genre and then reads the genre, pretending to be a member of that audience. Next, to help focus this initial response, ask each student to do the following:

1. Read through the genre. Based on what you know about the genre, comment on what's working and what needs attention.
2. *For writing students who have done Toulmin charts:* Outline the main claim, warrant and back-up, reason(s), support, counterargument, and rebuttal in this genre. Are there any parts missing? Justifiably, or not? Based on this skeletal frame, how well did the writer get his message or claim across?
3. *For literature students who have not used formal argument terminology:* Identify the main point and how the writer supports that claim.
4. Based on this genre, what should the writer do elsewhere in her choice of genres?

Using this activity several times during the writing process keeps students on track and helps them focus on small segments of their MVA at a time. If any genres are off target, students still have the opportunity to revise before the final assignment is due.

To give effective feedback on a complete draft, students need guidance. This exercise helps writers test-drive their drafts, and it gives useful advice to peer reviewers:

"Dear Reader" Letter:

Write a letter to potential readers of your project, telling them why you wrote it the way you did. "Readers" here refers to people who might actually read your paper—such as your teacher and classmates—not the hypothetical audience you are envisioning to help you focus your paper.

If you have questions about your draft, such as whether a particular genre is appropriate, or even whether you have enough information, include those questions as part of your letter. (You could do this by saying "Now I'd like to ask you some questions about what you see when you read my paper. . . . ")

After you have finished writing your letter, give your peer reviewer a copy of your paper, but don't let the reviewer see your "Dear Reader" letter yet. First, have your reviewer read through the MVA carefully and jot down what seems to be the thesis, major support, and general purpose of the paper. Then the reviewer should evaluate the effectiveness of the individual genres and how well they work together, and determine the project's greatest weaknesses and strengths.

After your reviewer reads your paper, ask the reader to also read your letter. If your reviewer did not see all that you hoped, discuss together ways of making your MVA more effective.

Doing a "Dear Reader" letter gives writers a chance to clarify their thoughts. Many students use this piece later on as the basis for the "Rationale" that they write to accompany their completed project.

Students who understand the strategies involved in multigenre and multivocal writing can give each other valuable feedback on their drafts and learn valuable lessons themselves in the process. For example, when Melanie's classmates read her draft, they really liked what they saw. But they did not feel comfortable with the language Melanie had used in the letters she wrote in the voice of Rev. Albright. They thought those letters seemed "too nice!" When they read in Melanie's "Dear Reader" letter that she had intended these letters to be full of righteous indignation, they knew they needed more work. Melanie herself appreciated this advice. As she says in her "Rationale," she found it hard to strike the right tone and to find the appropriate vocabulary in these letters. She felt that the reverend's point of view was just too different from her own. With the help of her classmates, however, Melanie revised the piece to make it far more effective. Having experienced first hand the importance of striking the proper tone, Melanie's reviewers were able to look at their own MVAs with a more objective eye.

The Value of Process Work

We credit our students for taking risks and for paying explicit attention to the process of writing. We might, for example, require our students to workshop a list of genre choices, hand in their Toulmin charts, and produce drafts of at least four genres. We reward them for their effort in these process writings by assigning points for each task, keeping these process points separate from the product grade. We want to show students that all of the writing they have done to create the MVA is valuable, even those pieces that did not ultimately succeed. All process work, however, must demonstrate a thorough and deliberate attempt to complete that assignment. Thoughtless or incomplete work does not receive full credit. This emphasis on process encourages students to complete a rich and sophisticated MVA.

Evaluating and Grading the MVA

In workshops we've conducted, teachers often express concerns about how to grade an MVA. We might feel comfortable evaluating an article or editorial but evaluating a poem might challenge us, especially if we've never taught poetry before or written a poem ourselves. A quick overview of our reading and evaluating processes may put grading into perspective.

Jen's and Melanie's MVAs

Here is the procedure we used to read and grade the papers of Jen and Melanie.

We both follow a similar pattern:

1. We quickly browse through the MVAs, noting particular traits. For example, Cheryl, Jen's teacher, noticed right away that Jen had shaped the piece as a packet of materials for *Disordered Media, Inc.,* "a foundation dedicated to the awareness of the media's presentation of women and the degrading effects it generates." This helped Cheryl understand Jen's audience and what she hoped to accomplish with the piece. Jayne had to read Melanie's MVA differently since it offers no notes or instructions to the reader. Leafing quickly through the pages that Melanie submitted, Jayne sees various email messages as well as other genres. The only way to find out what's going on is to start reading and let the story unfold.

2. We then read the entire document, trying to make sense of the argument presented from various angles. Next, we read the

writer's "Rationale" and return to the MVA for a second reading, keeping in mind what the writer sees herself doing in the text and measuring her intent against her actual accomplishments.

3. We apply the criteria on the Evaluation Grid and begin to formulate a composite decision.

4. Finally, we record our totals on the grid, explain why the student was awarded points for a certain criteria, and add a summative comment for the entire project.

Since we are focusing on argument in different classes (writing and literature), we design our evaluation grids to fit our particular assignments. A sample grid might include the following criteria included in the example in Figure 4-1.

Many of these expectations are similar to what we expect of traditional researched arguments. If we make these criteria clear, then the grading process will become clear to our students, enabling them to see that the grades they received are earned.

Specific Concerns Related to Jen's Paper

Cheryl did not know that Jen had suffered from eating disorders until about three weeks into the project. Passionate about her choice of issue, Jen needed time to know if she could trust her instructor. Only then did she decide to use diaries as a window to her personal experience. Jen warns us in her preface that "some of the material may be extremely revealing and emotionally stimulating" and asks us to "please remember that this is a serious problem with severe, even life-threatening consequences." Her diary sequence begins on the very next page. This is true risk-taking: Jen is laying out her problem from nearly page one, a problem that she hid in the closet for years and is only now ready to understand, establishing her credibility by showing that she's critically examining her own life. By her final diary entry, she is reflecting not only on her own life experiences but also on what she's discovered through research. In short, her perspective deepens, partly because she *is* writing in different genres from different points of view, including diary entries that reflect what it is like to be in the mind of this writer.

Jen created a project that is clearly an "A" paper for us, having satisfied most of the criteria above, though losing a few points in three categories: development of thesis/use of supporting evidence; research; and organization/unity. Despite having constructed a full Toulmin chart as one of her required process-writings, Jen's final project still needs a stronger appeal to logos. Her MVA would have been stronger if she had addressed the warrant that underlies her claim that media images damage self-esteem, instead of taking for granted that

Figure 4-1
Sample Evaluation Grid for the MVA

MVA Evaluation

Audience-Awareness and Development of Thesis/Use of Supporting Evidence:

➤ The writer significantly answers his/her problematical question through the use of the genre(s).

➤ The writer narrows, defines, and clarifies the central purpose/question for this essay.

➤ The writer's main point/thesis aims at the intended audience and is clear after reading the entire project; it may or may not be explicitly stated.

➤ The writer constructs an effective argument with credible appeals to logos, ethos, and pathos.

➤ In each genre, the writer uses supporting material from the interview and outside sources to advance and argue for the central thesis.

➤ By the end of the paper the reader sees that the writer has presented an argument.

Research

➤ The project reflects serious, in-depth research.

➤ The writer appropriately uses six to eight sources.

➤ The writer avoids plagiarism and appropriately documents and explains the sources used.

Genre-writing

➤ The writer has written competently and thoroughly in the chosen genres and voices.

➤ The genres are appropriate for the audience and the purpose of the project.

➤ The writer included at least five genres.

(continued)

Figure 4-1
(*continued*)

Organization/Unity

➢ The project is clearly and effectively organized and forms a unified whole.

➢ The sequence of genres makes sense and meets the needs of the reader.

Surface Errors

➢ The paper has few editing or proofreading errors.

➢ The writer's usage, grammar, sentence structure, and punctuation are clear and correct or appropriate when a specific genre requires nonstandard usage.

Rationale

➢ The writer includes a complete and fully explained rationale.

Process Materials
(These points are separate from the paper grade)

The writer included the following in-class and homework assignments. The work is thorough and thoughtfully completed.

➢ Two rough drafts of genres with reader's critique stapled to each one

➢ List of genres, voices

➢ Example of a genre plus analysis

➢ Complete Toulmin chart

➢ Definition of key term and an analogy

➢ Full definition of your audience, persuasive goal, and exigence

➢ In-class exercise on Toulmin method and appeal to logos

➢ Photocopied sources required (not here, no credit for project)

Reader's Critique
(These points are separate from the paper grade)

➢ The writer responded to the "Dear Reader" letter of another writer thoroughly and completely.

her audience will accept this idea without question. For the most part she uses research well, but the information she obtained in an interview she conducted with one of her instructors, who was also the father of a young girl of the age that Jen considered the most vulnerable to the media's messages, is included in only one of her genres and marginally even there. A father's perspective and the information she received from him could have enriched other genres, such as the lesson plan at the end of her MVA. By including the lesson plan in her project, Jen appealed to her readers, especially teachers. She still needs to work on writing that particular genre well, but what stands out is that it doesn't effectively connect to her previous genres. She needs a hook, a reason for its place in that particular spot in her MVA. Even though students are writing in genres we may not have taught in class (e.g., a lesson plan), they are still responsible for writing an effective piece and making it cohere within the whole. Jen's citing of sources could also be improved. Her Works Cited page does not reflect all the sources she refers to on her Notes page.

Specific Observations Related to Melanie's Paper

Because Melanie had studied with Jayne in a previous course and worked with her on the campus literary journal, Melanie felt comfortable enough to consult with her often during the writing process. Moreover, Melanie felt *so* comfortable that she did not hesitate to let Jayne know, at great length, that she really did *not* want to write a multivoiced argument at all.

Melanie based her objection to the MVA on having done a project in another class that was called a multigenre research project, but lacked our strenuous research requirements. Melanie was convinced that the MVA would turn out to be "lightweight," too, even though she resisted the notion of incorporating research into her genres—the very thing that would give the project substance. If we wanted her to do a "creative" project, why not just let her be creative? She called the MVA, in fact, "a creative project with footnotes" that wasn't academic enough to be respectable. About halfway through the process, however, Melanie told Jayne that not only did she not hate doing the MVA as she had anticipated, but she loved it! In fact, in her final "Rationale" she wrote, "I started to see how valuable it was, because it gave me the opportunity to show a variety of perspectives within one paper. And once I realized that I had probably done twice as much research for my MVA as I usually do for a traditional paper, I dismissed the idea that the MVA wasn't academic!"

Why is the student's attitude relevant here? Because Jayne was genuinely surprised when she saw the final product, even though she had seen parts of it, in isolation, before. Melanie eventually told Jayne that even when she had formed her basic concept and begun planning her project, she was mentally protesting all the way. It was only when Melanie became deeply involved in the research that she started to appreciate the MVA as a concept and grew excited about the possibilities it afforded her.

Though a very different type of MVA from Jen's and certainly not perfect, Melanie's project earned an "A." There were some weaknesses, but Jayne believed that they did not undermine its overall effectiveness. Reading the MVA, Jayne could see that Melanie had worked hard to present each side fairly and objectively, even though she held her own strong views. But Jayne was not entirely convinced that readers would automatically see, as Melanie claimed in her "Rationale," that her thesis is overtly stated in the student paper "One Step Closer to Gilead," since it is not quite clear if Melanie supports the views expressed in that essay. Jayne also wished that Melanie had used additional sources in Ms. Johnson's article on teaching *The Handmaid's Tale*. The only suggestion Jayne had for organization/unity was to refer to "One Step Closer to Gilead" in another genre. For example, she could have had Mollie indicate in email to Sarah, "Wow, my classmate Bianca wrote the coolest term paper on *The Handmaid's Tale*. It's spooky because it reminds me of exactly what my own dad is doing here!" Jayne also thought that the project was remarkably free from surface errors, the final category on which students in this class were evaluated. Melanie edited and proofread quite carefully, which Jayne felt was a personal victory for Melanie, who in earlier papers had quite a few of what Melanie called "comma issues." This improvement may well have been a result of Melanie's significant investment in this writing project.

MVAs are indeed often a great pleasure to read, but like any other assignment, they do not all achieve genius. The kind of pedagogy we have been describing will only succeed to the degree that students, instructors, and administrators understand that it can be evaluated in ways that are rigorous and fair. Measuring good writing is a complex process. No one set of activities will fully unravel our complicated roles as teachers. Chris M. Anson (1989) writes of our creative "schizophrenia" as teachers. We are at once the "helpful facilitator, hovering next to the writer to lend guidance and support, and now the authority, passing critical judgment on the writer's work; at one moment the intellectual peer . . . at the next the imposer of criteria, the gatekeeper of textual standards" (2). Recognizing this rich interplay of roles and knowing that an element of risk haunts teacher and student interactions should temper our attitudes toward student texts. What we strive for is a balance between encouraging students to take risks and holding them accountable for their choices.

Chapter Five

Reflections and Sources for Further Learning

Our own stories, as coauthors and as teachers, show how teaching multigenre arguments affected our professional lives. When we started teaching academic writing, we saw ourselves as the engineers of a train. The Boxcar Queens. We thought that if we taught our students a pattern of ideas and strategies, they would create a trustworthy structure based on classical argument: the inverted triangle introduction with the major claim at the end, three mid-section paragraphs that marshaled out the reasons and strong supporting evidence, followed by a paragraph that nodded to the opposition in which students would show the weaknesses in the opponent's position, and the summative conclusion that strongly echoed the major claim. Hearing such a paper read out loud, a listener would pick up the flat, monotone voice of the writer, peppered with quotes from researchers.

Eventually, we derailed that train. We now see ourselves more like a Miles Davis trumpet piece, both improvised and structured, using many instruments to meld various tones and argumentative moves. Structure is still important in this arrangement; we may still use the Toulmin method to support how we ask students to construct arguments. But now our students explore writing in a variety of genres (even genres we identify as *creative* forms, like poetry, stories, and plays) from various perspectives.

We see a strong correlation between our personal lives and what happens in our writing classes. We are *women writers interrupted*—by genres and voices from our multi-layered lives, and these intrusions shape our discourse together and shape how we conceive argument in our classrooms.

Sometimes our "interruptions" are due to the typical things that one would expect a professor to have: a student who unexpectedly needs help, papers that have to be graded, countless emails, an unduly long committee meeting. More often, though, our interruptions have to do with other roles we fulfill as women. Our work is interrupted by a host of real-life priorities: sick children; children who need to be fed, put to bed, played with; children who must have clean underwear for school tomorrow; a grown son who needs an emergency babysitter for his son; or a daughter needing a long, two-hour telephone conversation.

These interruptions have become part of our daily lives, and our work together, as attested to by email messages with subject lines such as "NOT DONE!" "Back in an Hour," "Jackson's sick!" "Need more TIME," "New Plan," "Life Is a Nightmare," and "Guilty Me."

In our teaching lives, we *all* juggle multilayered lives and hear multiple voices in our heads. And we know our students similarly juggle different genres and voices in their daily lives. Assigning multigenre arguments in all their variations can help writers explore their own multiple identities and give them a chance to experience for themselves a kind of metamorphosis.

We invite our readers to visit the book's companion website, *www.boyntoncook.com/multiplegenresmultiplevoices*, on which we showcase more student examples of multigenre arguments and more activities that will help teachers construct their own projects.

Sources for Further Learning

For readers who want to investigate sources that will help in their thinking about and teaching of multivoiced and multigenre argument, here are some citations and brief annotations for books and articles we've found particularly valuable.

Allen, Camille A. 2001. *The Multigenre Research Paper: Voice, Passion, and Discovery in Grades 4–6*. Portsmouth, NH: Heinemann.
> Though focused on upper elementary students, Allen's step-by-step directions and mini-lessons for creating a multigenre project could be easily adapted to most classrooms. We've found her book immensely helpful and inspiring.

Ballenger, Bruce. 1998. *The Curious Researcher: A Guide to Writing Research Papers*. Boston: Allyn & Bacon.
> Ballenger combines a step-by-step guide to writing research with an invitation to student writers to write lively prose for a "research essay." We've adapted some of his many innovative exercises and have never been disappointed.

————. 1999. *Beyond Notecards: Rethinking the Freshman Research Paper.* Portsmouth, NH: Heinemann.
Ballenger presents the exploratory research essay (not the argumentative research paper), as a bridge between personal and academic writing, a true invitation to academic inquiry. We've found this book a thoroughly engaging discussion of the scholarship that underpins research writing, and we fully endorse Ballenger's desire to make inquiry the heart of true research. We believe that a multivoiced genre argument can fruitfully expand the dialectical process and engage student writers in variety of genres—personal, popular, and academic.

————. 2005. *The Curious Writer.* New York: Pearson Longman.
Ballenger stresses inquiry and discovery in his composition textbook for first-year writing courses. In the chapter on "Writing an Argument" he raises a key question about oversimplifying significant issues: "rather than either/or can it be both/and? Instead of two sides to every issue might there be thirteen?" (287). We couldn't agree more; his pedagogy on teaching argument will not only engage students but also will help teachers see and broaden the possibilities for designing argumentative assignments.

Bishop, Wendy, ed. 1997. *Elements of Alternate Style: Essays on Writing and Revision.* Portsmouth, NH: Heinemann.
In this edited collection of essays, Bishop showcases the work of innovative teachers who describe activities that have helped their students explore writing in fresh ways. This book is a goldmine for teachers open to exploring experimental writing that still meets the standards of good writing.

Bishop, Wendy, and Hans Ostrom, eds. 1997. *Genre and Writing: Issues, Arguments, Alternatives.* Portsmouth, NH: Heinemann.
This collection of essays explores "genre" from theoretical, critical, and pedagogical perspectives. Read this book to get a better background in, and understanding of, new concepts in genre and how they relate to student writing.

Bishop, Wendy, and Pavel Zemliansky, eds. 2001. *The Subject Is Research: Processes and Practices.* Portsmouth, NH: Heinemann.
Aimed at first-year college students, the contributors to this collection discuss innovative ways to approach research and research writing. See especially Part IV (Genre and Research) for four different chapters focused on alternative genres for student research, including your coauthors' chapter on multigenre research.

Freedman, Aviva and Peter Medway. 1994. *Learning and Teaching Genre.* Portsmouth, NH: Heinemann.

These coauthors give an informative overview of genres that students use in school settings. They examine how various contributors approach genre as social action in curricular decisions and classroom practices. One essay, "Learning to Operate Successfully in Advanced Level History" by Sally Mitchell and Richard Andrews, focuses on argument. The authors contend that successful argument depends on re-thinking the conceptual scheme that underlies a thesis and on experimenting with dialogic forms of argument (Socratic dialogue, letter exchanges, symposiums) which "might be closer to the spoken discourses that go on in classrooms and seminar rooms" (99–100). In short, they support using argumentative forms that connect to a real social context. This collection, exploring the teaching and learning of school genres, gives important background for writing teachers, both secondary and college.

Fulkerson, Richard. 1996. *Teaching the Argument in Writing.* Urbana, Illinois: NCTE.

Fulkerson addresses both high school and college teachers of composition and focuses on how to teach, analyze, and assess a variety of approaches to argument. He has an especially clear explanation of the Toulmin method.

Jolliffe, David. 1999. *Inquiry and Genre.* Boston: Allyn and Bacon.

Jolliffe uses a sequence of writing assignments, in a variety of genres, including an inquiry contract, a reflective reading response, an informative report, an exploratory essay, and a working-documents project that includes more than one genre in its composition. His approach helps students become aware of how genre shapes and is shaped by social contexts. They explore one issue and develop skills by creating a variety of texts. His book helps students and teachers expand their repertoire beyond the research essay or theme.

Lunsford, Andrea A. and John J. Ruszkiewicz. 2001. *Everything's An Argument.* New York: Bedford.

This book focuses on all kinds of arguments with real-life examples that are engaging and especially useful for students to see. You will find succinct definitions and explanations of key approaches to argument that will help you construct your own multigenre argument projects.

Mitchel, Sally and Richard Andrews. 2000. *Learning to Argue in Higher Education.* Portsmouth, NH: Heinemann.

The coauthors include two essays that explore genre writing in argument classes: "Teaching Writing Theory as Liberatory Practice" by Catherine Davidson and "Eager Interpreters: Student Writers and the Art of Writing Research" by Claire Woods. Davidson shows how students used a variety of forms (dialogue, journal writing, letters, etc.) to make arguments, and Woods shows how the use of narrative deepens ethnographic writing. Both writers open the door to innovative ways of seeing argument.

Ramage, John D. and John C. Bean. 1998. *Writing Arguments.* Boston: Allyn and Bacon.
This college textbook is an excellent rhetoric for understanding both the practice and theory of argumentation. It takes a process approach to writing and contains excellent apparatus to support each step.

Romano, Tom. 1995. *Writing with Passion: Life Stories, Multiple Genres.* Portsmouth, NH: Heinemann.
Romano offers his heart-felt rationale for engaging teaching with risk and exploration. He includes stories focused on his own teaching life, his personal life, and his own journey as a writer and reader. Two chapters focus on how he taught the multigenre research paper in his high school classroom as a researched exploration of a person. His work inspires us and is responsible for us *wanting* to develop our own approach, one that would match departmental definitions of rigorous academic writing.

———. 2000. *Blending Genre, Altering Style.* Portsmouth, NH: Heinemann. Though aimed at both in-service and pre-service English language art teachers, this book's focus on practical strategies for composing multigenre projects as an expressive art form that incorporates research proved invaluable. His many excellent student examples of projects and different genres and his discussion of them can easily be adapted to the college classroom. Romano is the guru of multigenre writing, and no one should miss reading him.

———. 2004. *Crafting Authentic Voice.* Portsmouth, NH: Heinemann. This book is a goldmine of reflections, musings, and practical strategies to help students discover and craft a variety of personae. Readers learn how to trust their "gush" and experiment with style. We highly recommend Romano, not only to help students improve their writing but to give teachers an enthusiastic and supportive writing coach.

Starkey, David, ed. 2001. *Genre by Example.* Portsmouth, NH: Heinemann. The contributors describe the limitations of traditional academic genres and encourage teachers to experiment with genre forms designed to show that writing can be both creative and academic. For example, David Merger's "A Dialogue on Dialogues" presents a dialogue that explores inquiry as a form of knowledge and shows his readers how a dialogue exchange opens a depth of discussion that an essay might miss. The volume contains practical and specific strategies for including more imaginative writing in our existing classes.

———. ed. 1998. *Teaching Writing Creatively.* Portsmouth, NH: Heinemann. Starkey encourages us to risk teaching experiential forms of writing. This volume of essays offers authentic modeling and pedagogical advice; it is an excellent source for teachers using multigenre texts. See especially Sheryl I. Fontaine and Francie Quaas, "Transforming Connections and Building Bridges: Assigning, Reading and Evaluating the Collage Essay"; the collage essay complements our work on the multigenre argument. The collage essay establishes relationships between adjacent genres that, when combined, allow new connections to emerge.

References

Allen, Camille A. 2001. *The multigenre research paper: Voice, passion, and discovery in grades 4–6*. Portsmouth, NH: Heinemann.

Annas, Pamela J., and Deborah Tenney. 1996. Positioning oneself: A feminist approach to argument." In *Argument revisited; Argument redefined: Negotiating meaning in the composition classroom*, edited by Barbara Emmel, Paul Resch, and Deborah Tenney, 127–52. Thousand Oaks, CA: Sage.

Anson, Chris M. 1989. Response to writing and the paradox of uncertainty. In *Writing and response: Theory, practice and research*, edited by Chris M. Anson. 1–11. Urbana, Illinois: NCTE.

Bishop, Wendy, ed. 1997. *Elements of alternate style: Essays on writing and revision*. Portsmouth, NH: Heinemann.

———. 1997. Preaching what we practice as professionals in writing. In *Genre and writing: Issues, arguments,* alternatives, edited by Wendy Bishop and Hans Ostrom, 3–18. Portsmouth, NH: Heinemann.

Bishop, Wendy, and Hans Ostrom, Eds. 1997. *Genre and writing: Issues, arguments, alternatives*. Portsmouth, NH: Heinemann.

Bridwell-Bowles, Lillian. 1992. Discourse and diversity: Experimental writing within the academy. *College Composition and Communication* 43 (3): 349–68.

Council of Writing Program Administrators. 2000. WPA outcomes statement for first-year composition. *www.council.org/positions/outcomes.html* (accessed by authors 25 March 2004).

Davis, Robert and Mark Shadle. 2000. 'Building a mystery': Alternative research writing and the academic act of seeking. *College Composition and Communication* 51 (3): 417–46.

Freedman, Aviva and Peter Medway. 1994. *Learning and teaching genre*. Portsmouth, NH: Heinemann.

Gage, John T. 1996. Reasoned thesis: The e-word and argumentative writing as a process of inquiry. In *Argument revisited; Argument redefined: Negotiating meaning in the composition classroom*, edited by Barbara Emmel, Paul Resch, and Deborah Tenney, 3–18. Thousand Oaks, CA: Sage.

Heilker, Paul. 1996. *The essay: Theory and pedagogy for an active form*. Urbana, Illinois: NCTE.

Kroll, Barry M. 2000. Broadening the repertoire: Alternatives to the argumentative edge, *Composition Studies*. 28 (1): 11–27.

Lamb, Catherine E. 1996. Feminist responses to argument. In *Perspectives on written argument*, edited by Deborah P. Berrill, 257–69. NJ: Hampton.

Leonard, Elisabeth Anne. 1997. Assignment #9: A text which engages the socially constructed identity of its writers. *College Composition and Communication* 48 (2): 215–30.

Romano, Tom. 1995. *Writing with passion: Life stories, multiple genres.* Portsmouth, NH: Heinemann.

———. 2000. *Blending genre, altering style.* Portsmouth, NH: Heinemann.

———. 2004. *Crafting authentic voice.* Portsmouth, NH: Heinemann.

Schroeder, Christopher, Helen Fox, and Patricia Bizzell. Eds. 2002. *Alt-Dis: Alternative discourses and the academy.* Portsmouth, NH: Heinemann.

Starkey, David. 2001. *Genre by example: Writing what we teach.* Portsmouth, NH: Heinemann.

Young, Art. 2003. Writing across the curriculum. *College Composition and Communication* 54 (3): 472–85.

Appendix A

This appendix contains an assignment sheet for the MVA and two sample MVAs: "The Feminine Ideal: Women in the Media," by Jen and "Gilead Revisited: A Contemporary Tale of Censorship in America," by Melanie. Because of space limitations, some genres in Jen's and Melanie's projects were excluded. We will note these exclusions in their projects as they occur, and you can find their full projects on the book's website, *www.boyntoncook.com/multiplegenresmultiplevoices.* We also include the "Rationale" form that teachers can use to help them devise their own projects. We describe both students' goals and processes in writing these projects in Chapter 2. Though these projects are longer and more complex than the average MVA, we chose to include them because they clearly illustrate the strengths of this approach to argumentative writing. We also refer to these two projects in Chapter 4, where we explain how to evaluate the MVA.

Since we often devise at least one assignment that precedes the MVA, we also include suggestions for preliminary assignments on the book's website. More sample MVAs and Jen's and Melanie's complete "Rationales" are also on this website. Such work supports the MVA and often helps students create stronger projects.

MVA Assignment Sheet

The following assignment sheet for a capstone MVA contains the same basic elements as those completed by Jen and Melanie. We have removed many of the references to our own course content in an effort to make this material more adaptable. Literature classes typically exclude references to *pathos*, *ethos*, and *logos*.

The Multivoiced Argument Project

For this assignment, you will create a Multivoiced Argument (which I will refer to as a MVA) written to persuade a specific group of readers to think or act differently. Essentially, you will construct an argument using more than one genre and more than one voice to express your understanding of an issue or problem. You should present your issue or problem from various points of view, not just from one perspective, although by the time the reader reads all parts of your paper, your central point should be clear.

You'll need to construct a multivoiced argument that

- Builds and structures an approach to argument, using one of the different approaches to argument we've discussed in class or a combination thereof
- Meets the needs of a specific audience, which you define
- Appeals to the emotions (*pathos*) and interests of your audience so they will act in response to your persuasive goal
- Appeals to your own good sense, wisdom, and connection to your writing situation (*ethos*) so that your readers will act in response to your persuasive goal
- Appeals to your readers' reasoning and patterns of thinking (*logos*) so that they will act in response to your persuasive goal
- Includes a minimum of three different voices and six genres in your paper, with at least two from group one. (See the genre charts on pages 19 to 20 for possibilities.)
- Integrates your sources *into* these genres. A total of eight written sources *plus* your interview are required.

  In addition, you will need to:

- Write a *two-page "Rationale"* and description that explains how you used your sources, how you created a unified piece, and what impression you intended to make on your readers, a group you'll also need to define. I will give you a list of questions which will help guide you through the rationale.
- Write a "Notes" page for this project (instead of the MLA in-text documentation). I will guide you through that process once you are further along.
- Include a "Works Cited" page at the end of the project.
- Hand in *all* your Xeroxed written sources.
- Complete all process assignments.

"Rationale" Form

Jen and Melanie used guidelines similar to these when writing their "Rationales."

Rationale for the Multivoiced Argument Project

Please answer the following questions and turn in with your MVA.

1. What is your research question and persuasive goal?
2. Who is your audience for this project? Describe in detail.
3. What do you most want readers to see in your project? How did you get this "thesis" across?
4. How did you choose your genres and why are they appropriate for your audience and persuasive goal?
5. How do the genres work together to form a unified whole? How did you determine what types of transitions to use between sections of the paper and what types of strategies did you use to achieve unity and clarity?
6. How did you use your written sources (including the required interviews) in each of your genres, and why did you choose to do it this way?
7. Where did you take the most risks?
8. What do you like best about your paper?
9. What would you improve if you had more time?
10. Offer advice for new readers of multivoiced texts. How might they best make sense of your multigenre project? Offer advice on how to enter your text, how to survive the process of reading it, and how to come out on the other side with understanding.
11. Compare your style and approach to other argumentative essays you have written. How does the writing process you used in the MVA compare to how you usually argue in other papers? How does the multigenre style shape how you see yourself as an arguer?
12. What am I not seeing in this paper or in your packet that you'll turn in? Maybe you did other genres that you didn't include; explain why. Maybe you suffered hugely. Maybe you struggled with procrastination. What's the behind-the-scenes drama that's not visible?

The Feminine Ideal:
Women in the Media

By Jen Eliopulos

Disordered Media, Inc.

Welcome to Disordered Media, Inc. We are a foundation that promotes awareness of the media's degrading images of women.[i] DMI was established in 1985 and strives to publicize the connection between disordered eating trends and the media. Our goal is to call attention to the plague of unrealistic images plastering billboards, fashion layouts, and advertisements that ultimately encourage eating disorders in many women. These images represent the standard of beauty in today's society and promote a physical investment to measure success rather than intelligence or ability. Our goal is to call attention to the facts; our mission is to tackle these disorders by the means the messages of thinness were primarily received—through the media.

One of the first steps in combating this corruption is to educate the public. It is imperative that you know what eating disorders are, how to identify the symptoms and the health implications, how to approach a friend, and how to approach the subject with others. We believe that the other mandatory defense mechanism against this pervasive disorder is the media itself. The problem is that eating disorders, like anorexia nervosa and bulimia, are private problems. They are not publicized like lung cancer and smoking. When was the last time you saw a campaign that boldly announced the health indications of disordered eating? If you did, was it impressionable? Did it make you want to make a change? If not, consider the consequences the uneducated public might suffer if they experiment in the destructive world of disordered eating.

Remind yourself that this problem *does* apply to you. Even if you do not suffer from an eating disorder yourself, or do not find the media images of women damaging, you most likely know someone who does. Join the fight—help us spread the knowledge and awareness:

- Know the difference between facts and myths about eating disorders, nutrition, and exercise. Knowing the facts will help protect you and those around you from inaccurate ideas, which may be used as excuses to maintain disordered eating patterns.
- Be honest. It won't help to avoid addressing your concern!
- Talk to people. Share this information packet. Addressing the problem is the first step in our defense.

At the heart of our purpose is a call for change. We encourage all of you—parents, educators, and students—to invest your time and focus on these damaging images. Examine how these representations of women are influencing our everyday lives. The fact is, we must participate in advertisements when we view them—exactly what advertisers want us to do. Instead, let's invest this participation in other worthwhile endeavors.

Parents: Are you sure that your children are comfortable with their appearance? Do you talk to them about weight issues? Do you talk to them about what they see in advertisements, on television, magazines, or any other form of media?

Educators: Are you informed of the problem that disordered eating causes? Are you prepared to teach the ethics of media images with full knowledge of the implications?

Students: Do you feel the pressure to mold to a body type different from your own? Do you read *Glamour, Seventeen, Cosmopolitan,* or *Maxim*? Have you, or has someone close to you, recently dieted to lose weight? Do you worry about being overweight? Do you, or does someone you know, suffer from a poor body image?

Do any of you find yourself studying images of thin women, wondering what it would be like (or what it would take) to have that body type? Do you know someone who does? This is a serious issue; the associated problems are endless. DMI is here to address as many of those as possible.

This packet is a collection of articles, facts, real-life stories, interviews, and advertisements. Some of the material may be extremely revealing and hopefully even emotionally stimulating; please remember that this is a serious problem with severe, even life-threatening consequences. Woven in with the following material, you will find diary entries from a young girl. *Kerri Smith, a recovering bulimic, graciously offered her recorded thoughts and feelings to show us her roller coaster ride through her eating disorder. It is our hope that the reality of the material will call attention to elements pertaining to our cause. We hope to ultimately inform you of the facts and then introduce a call for change. Your participation is crucial; please take the time to read and understand this packet. Thank you.

*Names have been changed to protect identity.

Diary entry 10/95

Today I did it. I did that thing that I never understood. . . . I looked in the mirror today, and my face is getting fat. Why can't I have one of those tiny faces? Maybe I could exercise more—I don't even know why I did it. I was so hungry today. . . lunch just didn't cut it. Everyone went to McDonalds. I didn't want to be the only one who wasn't eating. Then after I did, I felt so fat. The thought never even popped in my head before, but suddenly the thought wouldn't go away. It was almost like I was challenging myself to do something I had never done. How easy it seems. It was weird; it took me a couple of tries. My eyes were watering so badly—I thought mom would notice the smeared mascara. I was so worried that someone would hear. So I turned on the fan and the radio. I'm kind of hungry again, though.[xix]

The Ideal of Female Beauty

Eating disorders and the connection to media exposure.

By Karen Jones

Women are socialized to value appearance more than their accomplishments. These images too quickly become the primary focus for many women. Ask yourself: What is beautiful? What constitutes an attractive person? Certainly, it is not completely the emotional and intellectual bearing of a person. The desire and need for beauty has become such a necessity in many lives. Intentional or not, we resort to rating others on a physical basis.

Women are placed strategically in magazine layouts and on billboards to sell products. And these women are judged. Time and again, advertisers strive to create images that create desire. A downward spiral emerges from the media as diseases like bulimia, anorexia, and compulsive exercising become rampant in the lives of many women—young and old. Innocent adolescent girls and women of all ages have resorted to these gruesome habits to achieve "the look" that hovers everywhere. Media messages are not improving. Rather, they are following a dreadful path to destructive behaviors.

These unrealistic images can emphasize what you are not—thin with a concave stomach and virtually no body fat, tall, and beautiful—instead of celebrating what you are. This emphasis ultimately penetrates self-esteem, as "thin" becomes the ideal beauty and high value for women in society.

So where does this leave us? A large number of girls and women, although not meeting formal criteria for an eating disorder, have partial syndromes: disordered eating seriously impairs many people.[ii] In a 1990 study, Irving found that women describe themselves as being less attractive and satisfied with their image after viewing images of fashion models. It has been suggested that some women develop eating disorders in part because of these pressures to conform to an unrealistic image. How can we draw these types of conclusions? Simple. Let's just look at the facts:

- Americans are subjected to 3,600 ads a day.[iii]
- Most fashion models are thinner than 98% of women.
- 80% of women are dissatisfied with their bodies.[iv]

The disordered eating effect does not seem coincidentally connected to the media. From this information alone, we can conclude that the rampant thinness in the insane amount of advertisements we witness has a hand in the dissatisfaction of women towards their bodies. From this data, we can sufficiently conclude that the mass media contributes to emotions and actions of women.

The average size of the idealized woman has become progressively thinner, stabilizing at 13% to 19% below physically expected weight. Models such as Kate Moss reflect a mere 2% of American women who naturally obtain that type of body frame and remain healthy.[iv]

Advertising creates a standard for our culture. Advertisers thrive in this mentality. They use images to sell ideas to consumers that "this product will make you look like this." Take shampoo, for example. The featured models almost always are slender and tall with long, silky hair. Our minds somehow make the connection that the product will help us achieve all of these physical features. And the idea remains so appealing that we buy the product. Media definitions of sexual attractiveness promote either extreme thinness or a thin waist with large hips and breasts. This cycle has created a fantasy world that we strive to be a part of, but in reality never will. We will not look like the "perfect" women in the ads. But somehow we are convinced if we use the product that *she* uses, we will achieve her looks.

The effects? A growing number of people in a culture fixated on thinness are picking up the disease that destroys self-image.

Karen Jones is a regular contributor to Women's Health.

For more information about eating disorders, check out **NEDO - National Eating Disorder Organization** 6655 S. Yale Avenue Tulsa, Oklahoma 74136-3329 (918) 481-4044 http://www.laureate.com/nedo-con.html

Who Suffers From Eating Disorders?

- Approximately 1% of adolescent girls develop anorexia nervosa.
- Approximately 2% to 3% of young women develop bulimia nervosa.
- Two percent of adults suffer from binge eating disorder.
- Some 90% of those with eating disorders are adolescents and young women.
- Bulimia is as high as 15% in college-aged women.
- Although the common perception is that eating disorders are most prevalent among white, upper middle class young women, recent research indicates that of those who suffer from eating disorders:
  - 1 in 5 are poor
  - 1 in 4 are non-white
- Teenagers with asthma, attention deficit disorder, diabetes, and other chronic illnesses are reported to experience eating disorders 2 to 4 times more often.[vi]

Children and Adolescents

- Eighty-one percent of 10-year-olds are afraid of being fat.
- Nine-year-old children associate silhouettes of larger figures as having fewer friends and being less well-liked.[iv]
- More than 50% of high school girls want smaller features.
- The onset of eating disorders peaks at ages 14 and 18, corresponding to the ages of changes in an adolescent female's body and the transition to college/leaving the family home.
- Sixty-six percent of high school girls and 17% of high school boys are on diets at any given time.
- In a study of high school students' weight control practice, in the 7 days before the survey, 49% of females and 18% of males had skipped meals to lose weight.
- One in eight high school girls has used vomiting as a "diet aid."
- Eighty percent of high school females and 44% of high school males have used exercise to lose weight.

College

- Twenty-two percent of college women reported binging once a week, using laxatives, diuretics, or vomiting to control weight

Diary Entry   5/96

All my friends are buying new clothes for summer. . . the kind in all the magazines. I don't have that kind of money; I can't even fit in those kinds of clothes anyways. I'm short and stubby. I've been weighing myself every day, three or four times a day. I just want to lose 15 more pounds. Then I would be perfect. Even though I've already lost 5 pounds, I still look fat. Most girls are 115 or 120 pounds—I'm 127. I wonder if all the other girls do what I do—they have to or else they wouldn't look like that.[xix]

<u>Warning Signs</u>

➤ Has your friend lost a significant amount of weight lately?

➤ Does she avoid eating meals or snacks when you are together?

➤ Does she categorize food into "good foods" and "bad foods?"

➤ Does she calculate calories and fat grams extensively and repetitively?

➤ Does she talk or worry about her weight or body shape?

➤ Does she enjoy exercise,[v] or does she do it because she feels like she has to?

Diary Entry   *8/96*

I went to my first day of college today. I felt like such an outsider. I was really nervous. Since I had to stay on campus, I had to eat there. I had to do somethin. . . so I got a seat in the SUB and ate. It calmed me down, and I just people-watched. There are so many pretty girls here. There's no way I can compete. No one will think I'm pretty. . . just plain. But I couldn't come home to get rid of the food, so it just sat in my stomach. I couldn't stand it. I just won't eat on campus anymore.[xix]

(See the book's website, *www.boyntoncook.com/multiplegenresmultiplevoices,* for an excluded brochure that includes information on defining and identifying bulimia and anorexia.)

Diary Entry 5/97

Guys suck. I was over at this guy's apartment, and they were all looking at a Playboy or something. They were talking about how awesome the girls bodies were—and how they would never marry someone with a gut or "thunder thighs." I said I was going to go outside for a smoke—it helps me to not be hungry—but instead I walked to my car. Didn't want anyone to see me cry. Then I went home to eat. Then I felt so shitty that I had just eaten so much that I ran upstairs to do my thing. And I thought I would try to quit doing this thing—how can I when I know that guys just want what they see in those magazines? I might not have a perfect face or anything, but I can get skinny. Just eight and a half more pounds. Maybe I should just not eat. I wonder if Mom and Dad are on to something. [xix]

Interview Excerpt:

Martha Einerson speaks about gender advertisements[vii]

Martha is an educator in the Department of Communications at the University of Idaho. She received her Ph.D. at the University of Kentucky in 1994; her primary area of study was Mass Communication. Since then, she has received her doctorate, with her primary area of study being Interpersonal Communication and Cognate Feminist Theory.

Teaching is the most rewarding aspect of my work and experience in the communications field. I practice a broad tradition of liberal arts communication; thus students experience a wide condition of knowledge exploration beyond social scientific studies. I practice critical thinking skills as a vital attribute in social understanding. Experience, interaction, and empathy combine to create understanding beyond simple answers. My teaching style allows and encourages students to view the world around them critically; they are encouraged to push the limits in their learning and to question simple answers. I also use writing techniques in the classroom as I believe it is a fundamental means to sharing experience, meaning, interaction, and stimulation to class discussion[viii].

I've been talking to my students about culture and femininity in my Gender and Communication course. I strive to highlight how femininity is sold in our culture. From hairdo's to faces to bodies and body parts, we use (and abuse) these images to ultimately do what? Yeah, to sell products. I mean, look at any advertisement in <u>Cosmopolitan</u> or <u>Vogue</u>. Bodies are used to sell products. Each advertisement insinuates that using this product will make you beautiful and feminine, like the woman in the picture. Because of this, we participate with advertising and advertisers to construct definitions of femininity, masculinity, and gender. Even if we reject these images we see plastered everywhere, we still have to participate in them in order to process the message being sent. Do you see where I'm going with this? Think about how powerful these images are, and then think about how we can begin to view these ads critically to understand the context of the message. Try to look at it in a new light. Through my years of research and experience in the field, I've gathered really interesting, powerful concepts to formulate a definition of femininity:

Femininity means difference.

FEMININITY	IS DIFFERENT THAN	MASCULINITY
White femininity	is different than	*femininity born of color*
Heterosexual femininity	is different than	**homosexual femininity**
Rich femininity	is different than	*poor femininity*
Professional femininity	is different than	**domestic femininity**[ix]

I think students can really make a difference. They can definitely become aware and approach things differently because they have an educated grasp on ethics. But I think we have to increase a positive representation in advertising so it is more diverse, more fair to view. Until we get more voices to inject change, then it just won't change. As a professor, I am very adamant about the need for students to understand media literacy. If people can begin to view images critically, then this deeply rooted system may show change. There's been a lot of talk about adding Visual Media Literacy to the curriculum; it's definitely a step in the right direction. And, you bet, I'm there pushing for it.[x]

"Femininity is thin, white, heterosexual, made-up, high-heeled, soft, athletic, healthy, sexual, kind, caring, in competition with other females, mothering, submissive and domineering, smart but not too smart, indecisive, irrational, and always available."[ix]

(See the book's website, *www.boyntoncook.com/multiplegenresmultiplevoices*, for Jen's next two excluded genres: a set of journal entries that explore how the narrator avoided exposure and finally sought help, and an article on how the media influences adolescent girls' self-images.)

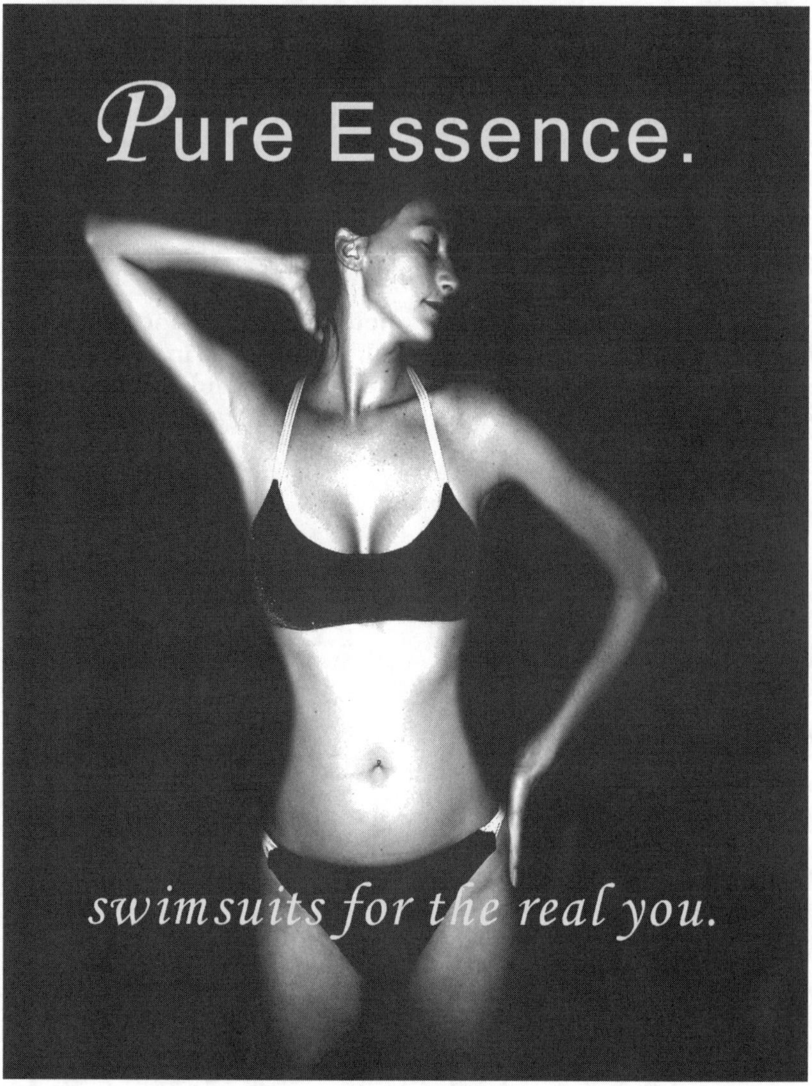
Pure Essence.
swimsuits for the real you.

1518 Stone Ridge Way
Moscow, ID 83843

April 5, 2000

Kids Today
17118 Fort Lane
Bozeman, MT 59715

Dear Editor:

I am writing in response to your April 2000 edition of *Kids Today*. I am outraged by the *Pure Essence* advertisement for swimwear. Your decision to feature this absurd material discourages my parental effort, as well as many others, to place appropriate and educational material in their hands. You have exposed sexual and unrealistic images to youth who are not emotionally or socially capable of processing messages safely.

Children's magazines should inspire them to do things; magazines for children should encourage them to be something; kids' magazines should inform them about important issues and what is going on in the world. Children's magazines should **not** inspire them to fixate on unrealistic portrayals of women; material available to children should not imitate what is rampant in women and men's magazines.

My primary concern for my daughter, who is approaching age 11, is that she will invest an unhealthy amount of her psychic, emotional, and physical energy in her body or image. I have agonizingly attempted to drive her from seeing her physical body as the central means of achieving power in our society. I have struggled with the idea that genetics will deny her of the popularized body she desires and she will damage her physical and/or emotional health attempting to realize that body. I fear that she will see the human body as a commodity, something that is bought, sold, and somehow exchanged for power, wealth, social acceptance, and security. You have reinforced all of these concerns for my daughter.

The featured advertisement for *Pure Essence* serves an illogical purpose in a children's magazine. I have terminated my subscription and will no longer endorse your company. I recommend that you begin to consider the negative effect your material is having on young children.[xiv]

Signed,

Tom Drake

Tom Drake[xv]

The Parental Detection: *How to know when our children have an eating disorder.*

Although it may be a difficult realization, it is important to know when our children are exhibiting symptoms of eating disorders. Poor nutritional habits, changes in eating patterns due to stress, and food fads are common problems for children. Furthermore, two psychiatric eating disorders, anorexia nervosa and bulimia, are on the rise among young girls and women. In the United States, 1 in 10 young women meet the formal criteria for an eating disorder.[xvi]

Parents should become familiar with symptoms of these disorders, although they may be hard to detect. Many young men and women successfully hide their patterns from their family and loved ones for months—even years. Despite this detour, parents can educate themselves by familiarizing themselves with the following information:

- A teenager with ***anorexia nervosa*** is typically a perfectionist and a high achiever in school. At the same time, she suffers from low self-esteem, *irrationally believing she is fat* regardless of how thin she becomes. Desperately needing a feeling of mastery over her life, the teenager with anorexia nervosa experiences a sense of control only when she says "no" to the normal food demands of her body. In a relentless pursuit to be thin, the girl starves herself. This often reaches the point of serious damage to the body, and in a small number of cases, may lead to death.

- The symptoms of ***bulimia*** are usually different from those of anorexia nervosa. The patient *binges* on huge quantities of high-caloric food and/or *purges* her body of dreaded calories by self-induced vomiting and often by using laxatives. These binges may alternate with severe diets, resulting in dramatic weight fluctuations. Teenagers may try to hide the signs of throwing up by running water while spending long periods of time in the bathroom. The purging of bulimia presents a serious threat to the patient's physical health, including dehydration, hormonal imbalance, the depletion of important minerals, and damage to vital organs.

Once detected, sufferers of eating disorders can be relieved of the symptoms or taught to control the disorder. Treatment usually includes the following:

- Individual therapy
- Family therapy
- Working with a primary care physician
- Working with a nutritionist
- Medication

Early detection usually results in a positive outcome. Parents, if you suspect that your child has an eating disorder, contact your local physician. He or she will recommend a psychiatrist for your specific needs (for children of specific ages).

Most importantly, do not ignore any symptoms your children have that may indicate that they have a problem. Remember, the earlier you get help, the sooner your children are off to a better, healthier attitude toward themselves and towards food.

This information sheet is brought to you by the American Academy of Child and Adolescent Psychiatry (AACAP). We currently represent 6,900 child and adolescent psychiatrists who are physicians with at least five years of additional training beyond medical school in general (adult), child, and adolescent psychiatry.[xvi]

Teachers Weekly, August 2000

Self-Esteem Builders:
methods to improve our students' self-image.

Lesson Objective:
Strategies for teachers to use to help raise student self-esteem.

Grade Level and Subject Area:
All grades. Any subject area.

Teachers: the following list provides suggestions for helping your students feel more secure about themselves.

- Use student names
- Shake hands with the students
- Have conversations with every student
- Provide multiple ways for students to be successful in your class
- Display student work
- Give each student a responsibility in the classroom
- Provide opportunities for student work to be judged by external audiences
- Take time to point out positive aspects of your students' work
- Never criticize students' questions
- Take time to help struggling students understand the material
- Try to discover what your students' lives are outside of school
- Ask students about their other activities (e.g., "How was the soccer game, Natalie?")
- Help students turn failure into positive learning experiences
- Encourage students to take risks
- Provide opportunities for students to make their own decisions about certain aspects of your class—maybe what kind of paper to use, what colors to make something, etc.
- Provide opportunities for students to work with each other
- Don't make assumptions about student behavior
- Allow students to suffer the consequences of their behavior—don't be overprotective
- Allow students to explore options in different situations
- Celebrate your students' achievements, no matter how small[xvii]

A Teacher's Perspective:

Recognizing symptoms in the classroom

By June Whetherly
Teacher, Prima Junior High, Escondido, California

I am writing to all teachers and educators out there. It is vital that we acknowledge and address issues surrounding eating disorders in students. Six months ago, I was naïve to the whole issue. Now I want to speak out and share my story with you.

Last fall, one of my female students, age 14, began showing signs of depression, low self-esteem, and strange eating behavior. I wasn't sure where the problem was rooted—family life, friend troubles, boy issues—I wasn't sure if I should approach the problem at the time. I decided to sit back and observe before I made any decisions.

Amy* was a good student. She excelled above the rest of the students. She consistently received good grades and was one of the most popular girls in her class; everyone looked up to her. I noticed that Amy had dropped a significant amount of weight. I had not realized this before. She always brought a brown paper bag for lunch, which always contained two baggies: one baggie was for sliced carrots, and the other one contained six celery slices.

I decided to discuss Amy's eating behavior with one of her closest friends. Her friend told me that Amy "wanted to lose weight," and that "she thought she was fat." This sparked an extreme sense of concern in me. I decided to talk to the school nurse.

Nancy Smith, a R.N. employed at our Junior High for six years, recommended that I contact the local psychiatrist and speak to him about Amy's symptoms.

The psychiatrist provided me with numerous brochures and information packets educating me about symptoms, effects, and treatments for eating disorders. This was the best possible action that I could have taken. Educating yourself, no matter who you are, is vital. It is important to learn about the different disorders and how to approach someone you suspect is suffering from one. Before reading these packets and brochures, I realize that I would have handled the situation inappropriately. It is important to understand that eating disorders are private; people who suffer from them often do not want to share their problems and feelings right away.

Over the next couple of weeks, I took several actions. The first step I took was to talk to Amy. I told her that she had been looking tired and

* Name has been changed for protection.

worn out over the past few months and that I was concerned. I reassured her that I would be available if she needed me. She told me that she was just tired and needed to catch up on her sleep. After watching her for the following month, I took her aside and suggested that she may want to see a doctor for a health assessment if she still wasn't feeling up to par (psychiatrists suggest using the word "assessment" instead of "therapy"). I told her that I knew a good doctor that specialized in teens and stress. I handed her his name and phone number.

When I took roll the following week, I noticed that Amy was not in her seat. My heart jumped right out of my chest. As I neared the main office, I felt sick to my stomach. I thought to myself, "If I had only taken action sooner." But my worries subsided instantaneously when the office secretary shared the reason why Amy was not in school: she had been enrolled in an eating disorder clinic that was run by the psychiatrist I recommended. I smiled and returned to the classroom.

It is my hope that this story inspires you to read and learn more about these terrible disorders. Anorexia and bulimia are on the increase in young girls; we as educators can help stop the rise by informing ourselves and those around us.[xviii]

Routes for Change: Utilizing the Media

By Rhonda Walters
Media Director, DMI

One of the reasons why eating disorders are an ongoing problem is because no one has really emphasized the medical implications. Sufferers of disordered eating experience an internal and external focus on their goal: decreased weight. This presents a problem because many medical problems are not evident; it is easier to ignore health problems associated with eating disorders because many are not visually evident. Anti-smoking campaigns have visually pointed out that smoking results in lung cancer. Posters are plastered everywhere—shouldn't we announce the harm eating disorders present to bodily health? But disordered eating remains a private problem. It remains the secret from the world for most individuals. Perhaps, a positive change—to help society advance towards change—would be to boldly address associated health risks.

Health is connected to physical and mental beauty. We can use it as a tool to help stop the deterioration of girls' self-images. Information, support, knowledge, education: they need to be emphasized and readily available.

Since American models play the role of "beautiful" in our society, we can also use them as a tool to place a shadow of doubt in the minds of the public. With the use of the "idealistic" woman (the model), we can emphasize the unhealthy nature of starving, bingeing, and purging to achieve the "look" of beauty as thin and tall. These visuals can help to implant a seed of knowledge, a link to unhealthiness instead of beauty, and a goal for people to help combat unrealistic images of women in the media. Then we can emphasize what good health is: we can stress good health on a healthy, normal, achievable body.[xx]

Rhonda Walters has been employed with Disordered Media, Inc. for eight years. Since then, she has implemented various successful media trends that have ultimately caught the public eye. She continues with her effort as we all strive for change.

(See the book's website, *www.boyntoncook.com/multiplegenresmultiplevoices*, for Jen's excluded final journal entry that shows how the narrator continues to battle the disease, as both a sufferer and as a consumer of ads.)

BEAUTY
is only
skin
deep...

HAIR LOSS

LONG HAIR
GROWTH ON
FACE AND
CHEST

REDUCED METABOLISM

HYPERACTIVITY   DRY SKIN

MUSCLE WASTING

SENSITIVITY
TO COLD

DEATH BY STARVATION

CONSTIPATION

DIGESTIVE DIFFICULTIES

REDUCED BODY
TEMPERATURE

...with
ANOREXIA.

BEAUTY is only skin deep...

HEADACHES, FATIGUE, IRRITABILITY

PUFFY FACE

BROKEN BLOOD VESSELS (IN FACE)

TOOTH ENAMEL EROSION

DEHYDRATION

LOW SELF-ESTEEM

RUPTURED ESOPHAGUS

HEART ATTACK

DEPRESSION

HEARTBURN

MENSTRUAL IRREGULARITIES

KIDNEY FAILURE

ELECTROLYTE IMBALANCE

...with BULIMIA.

Recommendation: A Proposal for Change

Disordered Media, Inc. has devoted its time and effort to educating the public about eating disorders; we strive to help students, educators, and parents to recognize the media's effect on self-image after subjecting us to damaging, unrealistic images. Our ultimate goal is to make a change. The following information contains our recommendations for redirecting this destructive trend.

Media messages may not be the direct cause of eating disorders, but they mold the context for people to place a value on physical features. Subsequently, the media should be encouraged to present more "real" body images (with body fat, hips and average height. Remember that fat on hips and thighs of women is healthy and vital for fertility; prevention of osteoporosis; healthy skin, eyes, hair, and teeth). Accompanied by positive messages related to health and self-esteem, this route may not be a guaranteed success for eliminating eating disorders, but it is the necessary step towards change. Altering the media's portrayal of the female body will help people feel better about their bodies. No longer will they be prone to depression because they don't conform to one ideal. This will lead to reduced feelings of dissatisfaction and, thus, decreased potential for acquiring an eating disorder. The following are recommendations for change:

- **Broadcasters and magazine publishers** should adopt a more responsible attitude toward the portrayal of extremely thin women as role models. They should begin to feature role models of various talents, abilities, and size ranges.

- **Advertisers** should consider their use of women with unrealistic body types to sell products; they should be more responsible with the implied connections or influences they are promoting. Advertisers should review their policy of using unrealistic models to sell products other than diet aids.

- **Health Professionals** should work hand in hand with advertisers and broadcasters to increase awareness of potential impact the programming may have on individual's eating habits & health. Health care professionals who work directly with women and children should be sure to discourage "dieting" (referred to as "restricting calories") unless absolutely necessary. Achievable goals should then be implemented.

- **School Curriculum** should include the critical viewing skills in order to interpret food advertising. Media Literacy programs should be implemented in grade schools through colleges.

- **Posters, fliers, and other informational forms** should feature the medical problems and risks associated with eating disorders. They should be highlighted in the public arena; risks should be visible in an attempt to emphasize irreversible effects and possible death through starvation and complications. Eating disorders should be presented for what they are—a significant cause of mortality and morbidity in young people, particularly young women. Even if young people recover from an eating disorder, they stand the chance of suffering from long-term health-related problems.[xxi]

Following these cues will create a healthier environment and more accurately portray women in the media; educate youth about critical viewing skills; highlight medical implications of eating disorders; and present less stress on an unrealistic body type. We need to unite to accomplish these goals; together we can offer an unbeatable defense and be less vulnerable to the media's powerful influences.

[i] Disordered Media, Inc. is a fictional corporation that specializes in eating disorders and their connection with the media's portrayal of women.

[ii] This information is gathered from an article from L.M. Irving (1990), entitled *Mirror Images: effects of the standard of beauty on the self-and body-esteem of women exhibiting various levels of bulimic symptoms.*

[iii] This information was given in my Ethics in Mass Communications course in Fall 1999 at the University of Idaho.

[iv] These statistics are from the following website: www.nmisp.org/eat/eat-fact.htm#body.

[v] These warning signs are in part from a brochure I picked up at the University of Idaho Student Health Center. It is entitled, "How to Help a Friend with Eating & Body Image Issues."

[vi] Statistics are from http://www.mirror-mirror.org/def.htm.

[vii] Martha Einerson is a professor in the Communications Department at the University of Idaho.

[viii] This is an interpretation of Martha's teaching philosophy

[ix] Martha Einerson's personal definition of femininity.

[x] I wrote this external monologue from her interview material to describe Martha's response to the difference that students can make when viewing and creating advertisements.

[xi] These statistics are from Commonwealth.

[xii] Information is collected from Guillen & Barr.

[xiii] Information from Levine, from the *Plenary Presentation at the Third Annual Eating Disorders on Campus Conference,* which was held at Pennsylvania State University.

[xiv] Material for this letter is directly from his answers to my list of 12 questions. Responses included his personal thoughts and fears for his daughter, who is in her pre-adolescent stage, and her confrontation with women in the media. He also responded with input about advertising in general, his viewpoint about appropriate media for young children, and his opinion about different "measures" of success within different age groups.

[xv] Tom Drake is an educator in the English Department at the University of Idaho.

[xvi] AACAP, the American Academy of Child and Adolescent Psychiatry, provides a framework of information for all areas surrounding eating disorders. This information is from a segment of the AACAP called *Facts for Families.*

[xvii] I received these strategies from the following website: http://education.indiana.edu/cas/tt/v3i2/selfesteem.html.

[xviii] This is a fictional story that I created about a teacher's perspective on eating disorders.

xix Each diary entry is a simulated collection of personal thoughts and feelings from a young girl—information is gathered from my personal experience with an eating disorder.

xx This is my interpretation of what needs to be done to make a change.

xxi These recommendations are from the *Plenary Presentation at the Third Annual Eating Disorders on Campus Conference,* which was held at Pennsylvania State University.

Works Cited

Coward, Rosalind. *Female Desires: How They Are Sought, Bought, and Packaged.* New York: Grove Press, 1985.

Eating Disorders Awareness and Prevention, Inc. *How to Help a Friend with Eating & Body Image Issues.* Seattle: 1989.

ETR Associates. *Eating Well and Looking Good.* Santa Cruz: 1996.

Garfinkel, Lin, & Goring. *Cultural Expectations of Thinness in Women. Psychological Reports,* 47, p. 483–491. 1994.

Goffman, Erving. *Gender Advertisements.* New York: Harper, 1976.

Irving, L. M. "Mirror images: Effects of the standard of beauty on the self- and body-esteem of women exhibiting various levels of bulimic symptoms." *Journal of Social and Clinical Psychology,* 9(2), 230–242. 1990.

Myers, P. N., Jr., & Biocca, F. A. The elastic body image: The effect of television advertising and programming on body image distortions in young women. *Journal of Communications,* 42 (3), 108–133. 1992.

Rakow, Lana A. *Don't Hate Me Because I'm Beautiful: Feminist Resistance to Advertising's Irresistible Meanings.* Kenosha.

Gilead Revisited:

A Contemporary Tale of Censorship in America

Melanie Cattrell

Contents

(This is a list of all the genres included in Melanie's MVA; some of them have been omitted here due to space considerations. The complete MVA can be found on the book's website, *www.boyntoncook.com/ multiplegenresmultiplevoices*.)

Email Message from Mollie Albright to Sarah Walker
"All About Me!"

Email Message from Mollie Albright to Sarah Walker
"Hey You!"

"Going Beyond Literature: Using Margaret Atwood's *The Handmaid's Tale* to Discuss Social and Political Issues in the Language Arts Classroom"
by Allison Johnson

Ms. Johnson's Creative Assignment Sheet for *The Handmaid's Tale*

Email Message from Mollie Albright to Sarah Walker
"Your Reading Pleasure"

Mollie's Creative Assignment
"Penalty for Perversion"
"Two Kinds of Freedom"

Email Message from Mollie Albright to Sarah Walker
"Big Problem"

Elmhurst Public Library Form For Reconsideration of a Work

Letter from Reverend Albright to Ms. Johnson

Letter from Ms. Johnson to Reverend Albright

Letters to the Editor

The Elmhurst Epistle

Letters to the Editor

"One Step Closer to Gilead: The Religious Right in America Today"
by Bianca Montgomery
Letter from the Director of the Elmhurst Library to Reverend Albright
Email Message from Mollie Albright to Sarah Walker
"New School"

Date: Wed, 12 Jan 2000 19:10:43 PST   <u>[Show full headers]</u>
From: "Mollie Albright"<MOLLIEPK@excite.com> [<u>Add to Address Book</u>]
To: Sarah_W83@excite.com [<u>Add to Address Book</u>]
Subject: all about me!

sarah!!

i'm so sorry i haven't e-mailed you lately! the past couple of days have been so busy . . . unpacking, going to a new school . . . i've barely had time to breathe! i miss you and the gang so much! today was my first day at elmhurst high. i'm taking about the same classes i was taking at lakewood—english, government, physics, trig . . . and 3 study halls! i guess senior year is the same no matter where you go. i was scared to death when i went to school this morning, but things weren't as bad as i thought. most of the people seemed really nice, actually. there were a couple of kids from church there— sami and becca, you would like them . . . becca wears her hair like you do, sarah . . . anyway, we all have the same lunch period, so i didn't have to eat alone! (that was my biggest fear!) anyway, those girls are sweet, but they seemed like they were acting a little too perfect in front of me, since i'm the new pastor's kid and all. for a second, i thought they were going to ask me to say grace for our macaroni and cheese, right in the middle of the cafeteria. boy, if they knew about some of the crap we used to do in Lakewood, they wouldn't have been so uptight!

my dad seems to be getting along pretty good here. i think it was good for him to get away from lakewood—too many memories of my mom there, i guess. i sometimes feel like we are trying too hard to forget her, and that's not what i want to do. can you believe she died two whole years ago, sarah? and we've only been to our new church twice, but i know some of the ladies in the church already have their eyes on my dad—eligible good christian man that he is, ha ha. i don't even want to think about him going on a date! that's just . . . ew, i can't even think about it!!!!

well i'd better go . . . would you believe those teachers gave me homework on the first day? the nerve!!

missing you!

mollie

(See the book's website for an excluded email message in which Mollie mentions how much she likes her new English teacher, Ms. Johnson.)

Going Beyond Literature:
Using Margaret Atwood's
The Handmaid's Tale
to Discuss Social and Political
Issues in the Language
Arts Classroom

Allison Johnson
Elmhurst High School

As English teachers and lovers of the art of literature, we are often so
focused on teaching our students the basic elements of fiction and
poetry, we forget that many works of literature cannot be easily cate-
gorized into our standard parameters of *plot/summary/character/
conflict/resolution*. Many literary works demand that we go beyond our
discipline and discuss political and social issues in our classrooms. As a
12th grade Language Arts teacher, I am always searching for novels that
are not only examples of excellent literature, but also that will make my
students more aware of the society around them. I believe that, as educators, we are obligated to teach our students to think critically about the
world that they are living in. By teaching Margaret Atwood's *The Handmaid's Tale* in my 12th grade Language Arts class, I am not only exposing
my students to a beautifully crafted novel, I am giving them the opportunity to examine numerous issues that were prevalent in the 1980s,
when Atwood's novel was written, and still exist in our society today.

THE DYSTOPIAN NOVEL

The Handmaid's Tale is often likened to Orwell's *1984*, the novel that
many of my colleagues use to introduce students to the dystopian form
of literature. I find that the dystopian form is powerful, because
through the dystopic lens, issues of freedom, choice, and control all
become startlingly clear. I choose to use Atwood's work instead of
Orwell's primarily because Atwood touches on many contemporary
social issues—such as feminism and homophobia—that are not found
in Orwell's work.

CONTEXUALIZING ISSUES IN ATWOOD'S NOVEL

The Handmaid's Tale is set in the Republic of Gilead, a theocratic dystopian society established in America's near future. As a result of a nuclear catastrophe, the majority of the residents of Gilead are sterile. Consequently, fertile women—including Offred, our narrator—are forced to become handmaids, women whose sole function in society is to bear children.

The Handmaid's Tale is a complex novel that is, in part, a reaction to the political atmosphere in America in the 1980s. Most of my students were born in the early eighties; they are too young to remember the political forces that were at work during that decade. Therefore, I begin the unit on *The Handmaid's Tale* by bringing in newspaper clippings and news footage from the eighties. Furthermore, when students enter my classroom, they are often only vaguely familiar with the principles of the women's movement, or with the history of women in America at all. Therefore, as a prelude to our reading of *The Handmaid's Tale*, we spend about a week discussing various women's issues. After we discuss the position of women in America today, we spend a couple of days focusing on the other minorities that exist in America. We discuss discrimination based upon race, ethnicity, sexual orientation, and economic status. (Is there a class system in America? If so, how do we know what class a person is in? Is our class system rigid, or does it have mobility?)

ENGAGING THE STUDENTS WITH THE TEXT

In order for Atwood's novel to impact my students, they must believe that a society such as Gilead could be possible. Atwood asserts that "there isn't anything in the book not based on something that has already happened in history or in another country, or for which actual supporting documentation is not already available" (317). To reinforce Atwood's claim, as we are reading *The Handmaid's Tale,* we make a list on the board of the different contemporary issues that are raised in the text. The issues mentioned vary from class to class; the ones that always appear are abortion (former abortion doctors are hung in Gilead); homosexuality (referred to in Gilead as "gender treachery"); feminism (Offred's mother is extremely active in the women's movement of the 1980s); environmental contamination (the sterility of the citizens of Gilead is a direct result of a nuclear disaster); and, of course, religion. Recognizing that the citizens of Gilead wrestle with the same issues that appear on the editorial pages of their daily newspapers brings Gilead closer to home for my students, and dispels the notion that Atwood's work could be dismissed as pure fantasy. After we have finished reading the book, I encourage my students to take on the persona of one or more of the characters in the text and to write poems, letters, or journal entries in the voice of their chosen character. I urge them to think about what social issues each character was forced to deal with and to incorporate these issues into their writings.

DEALING WITH POSSIBLE CLASSROOM OBJECTIONS TO ISSUES IN *THE HANDMAID'S TALE*

Some of my students are from conservative Christian backgrounds and have objected to my use of *The Handmaid's Tale* in the classroom. Most are uncomfortable because they feel the novel portrays Christianity in an unflattering—even mocking—light. While I can understand their apprehension, I firmly believe that Atwood's work is not against Christianity per se, but it is rather a warning that freedom cannot exist in a theocracy. As reviewer Stephen McCabe argued in 1986, "The novel's warning is not an indictment of the rising fundamentalist right as much as it is a warning to treat any repressive, regressive movement with truth and firm opposition early on. Acquiescence is our worst enemy." It is the acquiescence that McCabe speaks of that I am trying to combat by encouraging my students to become more aware of the issues that are prevalent in America today.

LITERATURE AS A SOCIAL FORCE

Literary texts such as *The Handmaid's Tale* are powerful not only because they serve as examples of excellent writing but also because they give us the opportunity to discuss issues in our English classes that are usually reserved for history or government classes. In order for our students to successfully integrate ideas and develop articulate and informed arguments, it is imperative that we, as English teachers, address social and political issues in our classrooms. By addressing numerous contemporary topics in one volume, Atwood's text gives us the perfect opportunity to do so.

Works Cited

Atwood, Margaret. *The Handmaid's Tale*. Anchor: New York, 1986.

McCabe, Stephen. "A Novel for the Complacent." Rev. of *The Handmaid's Tale*, by Margaret Atwood. *Humanist,* Sept.–Oct. 1986: 31–32.

Allison Johnson teaches English at Elmhurst High School in Elmhurst, Ohio. She also serves as the advisor for Emerging Voices, *the school literary arts magazine.*

Senior Language Arts
Assignment #12
Ms. Johnson
14 Febuary 2000

The Handmaid's Tale Creative Assignment

For our next assignment, we're going to try something a little different. You're going to step inside the mind of one of the characters in *The Handmaid's Tale* and write a poem, letter, diary entry, editorial, or essay from his or her point of view. If you want, you can write two different pieces from the same character, or the same type of piece from two very different characters. For example, you might want to write both an editorial and a diary entry from the Commander, showing that his internal beliefs are different from those that he shares with society. Or, you might want to write two poems by two very different characters in the book, like Moira and Aunt Lydia.

For this assignment, you must carefully analyze your chosen character/s. You may want to start by asking yourself questions about the character/s that you have selected. For example, if you were writing in Moira's voice, you might ask yourself the following questions: What type of language does she use? What is her attitude to those around her? How does she react when she is in danger? What motivates her? How is she different from Offred, or from Aunt Lydia?

I understand that some of you may have not done much—or any—creative writing before. Don't fret—I'm not expecting award-winning poetry here! I simply want you to produce a work that shows me you understand a specific character and his/her purpose in the novel.

Email me your idea no later than **Friday, the 18th**. If all goes according to plan, we'll workshop your rough drafts in class on **Wednesday, the 23rd**, and your final project will be due **Monday, the 28th**. As a celebration of our completed projects, we'll begin watching the film on the 28th! I'll bring popcorn with lots of butter!

As always, if you have any questions or problems with your assignment, come talk to me or email me as soon as possible!

(See the book's website, *www.boyntoncook.com/multiplegenresmultiplevoices*, for an excluded email message in which Mollie explains to Sarah that she has written the following two poems for her "creative assignment" for Ms. Johnson's Class.)

"Penalty for Perversion"

. . .God gave them over to their shameful lusts. Even their women exchanged natural relations for unnatural ones. In the same way the men also abandoned natural relations with women and were inflamed with lust with one another. Men committed indecent acts with other men, and received in themselves the penalty for their perversion. Romans 1:26–27

Then:
Scared and waiting
We knew something was about to happen,
There were too many people against us—
Too many people thumping their Bibles
And telling us we weren't natural.
But we never dreamed it would go this far.

Now:
Banished from breeder school
And trapped in this fucking funhouse
They created for girls like me
I got nowhere else to go

So, I just close my eyes and let them fuck me
Night after night
Sometimes, if their skin is soft enough,
I can close my eyes and pretend they are women

When it gets unbearable,
I just remind myself that
If I was a man,
I'd be hanging from a town square wall

Or in the colonies, wearing a gray dress
And shoveling nuclear death shit—
Compared with that, letting all these
Guys screw me ain't so bad, you know?

"Two Kinds of Freedom"

*. . .teach the older women to be reverent in the way they live, not to be slander-
ers or addicted to much wine, but to teach what is good. They can train the
younger women to love their husbands and children, to be self-controlled and
pure, to be busy at home, to be kind, and to be subject to their husbands, so that
no one will malign the word of God.*
Titus 2:3–5

These girls today don't understand
What we are trying to do
We are saving them

I was like them once
A stupid young thing who believed
I was free just because I

Dated any punk who asked me out
And went anywhere I wanted
Anytime I wanted

Thought I was making choices
And no one could stop me
I was asking for it, I was

Then I learned
Rules are made for a reason
You break them, you pay the price

The problem was with the women
Not with the men
We were messing with nature back then

We didn't want to admit we were different
We wanted to be like men
We thought they were just like us

We walked around half-naked
Practically inviting them to touch us
But cried rape when they did

What were we thinking, teasing
Them like that? We should have known
They couldn't handle it

But now we know better
And I won't let these girls
Make the same mistakes I made.

(See the book's website, *www.boyntoncook.com/multiplegenresmultiplevoices*,
for an excluded email message in which Mollie tells Sarah that her father
is very upset that Ms. Johnson assigned *The Handmaid's Tale*.)

Elmhurst Public Library
120 Main St.
Elmhurst, Ohio 44719
555-3623

Citizen's Request for Reconsideration of a Work

Author _Margaret Atwood_

Paperback_x_ Hardcover___

Title _ _The Handmaid's Tale_ _

Publisher (if known) _Bantam Doubleday_

Request initiated by _Reverend John Albright_

Telephone _555-3424 (work phone)_

Address _308 Main St. N.W._

City _Elmhurst_

Zip Code _44719_

Complainant represents
_X_ Himself/Herself

_X_ (Name organization)_Elmhurst Community Church_

____ (Identify other group)_____

1. Have you been able to discuss this work with the teacher or librarian who ordered it or who used it?
____ Yes _x_ No

2. What do you understand to be the general purpose for using this work?

a. Provide support for a unit in the curriculum?
____ Yes _x_ No

b. Provide a learning experience for the reader in one kind of literature?
_x_ Yes _No_

c. Other _____

Elmhurst Public Library

d. Did the general purpose for the use of the work, as described by the teacher or librarian, seem a suitable one to you?

____ Yes   _x_ No

If not, please explain.
The novel contains sexual situations that are not appropriate for young teenagers to read. There are many novels that would be more suitable for the classrooms and the libraries of young people.

4. What do you think is the general purpose of the author in this book?
To promote a left-wing feminist agenda.

5. In what ways do you think a work of this nature is not suitable for the use the teacher or librarian wishes to carry out?
The book presents a distorted picture of American life—it is anti-Christian, anti-American, and anti-family! It is pure liberal propaganda, and it does not belong in the hands of impressionable young people!

6. Have you been able to learn what is the students' response to this work?

____ Yes   _x_ No

7. What response did the students make?

Because of this book, my daughter wrote a poem that was filled with profanity and sexual content. This book planted ideas in the mind of my child that would not have been there if she had not been exposed to this filthy novel!

8. Have you been able to learn from your school library what book reviewers or other students of literature have written about this work?

____ Yes   _x_ No

9. Would you like the teacher or librarian to give you a written summary of what book

Elmhurst Public Library

reviewers and other students have written about this book or film?

____ Yes   _x_ No

10. Do you have negative reviews of the book?

____ Yes   _x_ No

11. Where were they published? _____

12. Would you be willing to provide summaries of the reviews you have collected?

____ Yes   ___ No

13. What would you like your library/school to do about this work?

_X_ Do not assign/lend it to my child.

_X_ Return it to the staff selection committee/department for reevaluation.

_X_ Other—Please explain

I demand that this novel be removed from the library _____ immediately!

14. In its place, what work would you recommend that would convey as valuable a picture and perspective of the subject treated?

Orwell's *1984*. It is a clear example of the dystopian form of literature, without the mindless feminist propaganda that fills the pages of Atwood's novel.

Signature *Reverend John Albright*

Date March 20, 2000

Elmhurst Community Church
310 Main Street N.W.
Elmhurst, Ohio 44719
555-3424

March 20, 2000

Ms. Allison Johnson
Elmhurst High School
320 State Street
Elmhurst, Ohio 44719

Ms. Johnson:

I am writing this letter out of the deepest concern for my daughter Mollie, as well as for her fellow classmates. I am extremely offended that you have chosen Margaret Atwood's *The Handmaid's Tale* as a required text for your 12th grade Language Arts class. Not only is the novel filled with sex, violence, and filthy language, it also repeatedly mocks and distorts the Christian religion. As a minister of the Christian faith, I cannot stand idly by and let the children of Elmhurst High School be subjected to such a novel.

Furthermore, not only do I object to the material that you are exposing the children of our community to, I object to the teaching methods that you are using in your classroom to engage the students in the novel. Upon reviewing my daughter's homework, I discovered that your last assignment was to have the students write poems from the perspective of a character in *The Handmaid's Tale*. In order to fulfill your assignment, my daughter wrote a poem that contained crude and profane language. When I discovered the poem and asked her why she used such profanity in a homework assignment, she explained to me that she was attempting to make her poem sound as though it were written by Moira, a character in the novel. When I asked her to describe the character of Moira to me, she explained to me that Moira was a rough-talking lesbian prostitute. I am shocked, Mrs. Johnson, that you would encourage your students to want to get inside the minds of such degenerate characters!

As a concerned parent, I simply cannot let such filth be encouraged in our school system. I have already petitioned the Elmhurst Public Library to remove *The Handmaid's Tale* from their shelves, and I strongly urge you to remove it from your classroom as well. If you refuse, I will be forced to speak to the school board regarding this matter.

Sincerely,

John Albright

Rev. John Albright

Elmhurst High School
320 State Street
Elmhurst, Ohio 44719
555-7632

March 22, 2000

Reverend John Albright
Elmhurst Community Church
310 Main Street N.W.
Elmhurst, Ohio 44719

Reverend Albright:

First and foremost, I would like to commend you for taking the time to write to me about Mollie's homework. It is obvious that you are concerned about the quality of the education that your daughter is receiving, and I applaud your concern. I hope to put your fears at rest by offering you a brief explanation of why I—and many of my fellow colleagues—believe that *The Handmaid's Tale* belongs in the language arts curriculum here at Elmhurst High School.

The Handmaid's Tale is taught in high school and college classrooms throughout the country. It is highly regarded as a compelling novel that not only teaches students about the dystopian form of literature, but also encourages them to examine and critique the society in which they live. I use the novel in my classroom not only because it is a genre of literature that many of the students have not yet been exposed to, but also because it raises many important issues about history, government, literature, and a variety of other disciplines. The novel is so rich that almost all of my students are able to connect with it on some level and are then able to relate it to their own personal interests and ideas.

While *The Handmaid's Tale* does contain certain situations which, taken out of context, appear to be sexual in nature, the book does not glorify or encourage sexual acts of any kind. Because most of my students are mature young adults, they were able to approach these portions of the book with tact and sensitivity. Furthermore, while the book does make numerous references to the Bible, Christianity itself is not being mocked in the novel; rather, the book is simply warning readers of the dangers of misinterpreting and misappropriating Scripture.

The Handmaid's Tale is a demanding and challenging book, yet Mollie and her fellow classmates handled the material well and exceeded my expectations. The students in her class—as well as Mollie herself—were all interested and engaged in the novel; many said that it was the most interesting book that we read all year.

Your letter also stated that you were concerned about the creative work that I assigned the students. Yes, I encouraged them to speak in the voice of characters in the novel, realizing that—depending on their character choices—such an assignment may require them to use language that is different from their everyday speech. However, the students were free to choose which character they wanted to speak; it was Mollie's choice to write in the voice of Moira. While I was surprised that Mollie chose to write from the point of view of someone who is so different from herself, I was impressed by the quality of her work. Her assignment was well written and convinced me that she understood the motivations of the character of Moira.

I hope I have put some of your fears about Mollie's assignment to rest. If you would like to discuss this matter with me further, please feel free to call me at school (555-3946 ext. 435) or at home (555-9731). If you would like to talk in person, just let me know, and we will schedule an appointment at your convenience.

Sincerely,

Allison Johnson

Ms. Allison Johnson

cc: Angela Williams, principal
        Frank Sloane, school board president

Letters to the Editor

Thank You, A&P!

I'd just like to thank the folks down at the Elmhurst A&P for always being patient with me! I'm 93 years old, but the folks at the A&P never seem to mind. Why, as soon as I walk through those front doors, all the cashiers smile and say "Hi Bertha," and the young men never hesitate to carry out my groceries, even when I only get something small like a can of tuna. Everyone is so friendly at the A&P, they almost make me feel like I'm back home in Whistle Stop!

Bertha Mason
Elmhurst

Downtown Parking Problem

While attempting to take my children to Story Hour at the Elmhurst Library last Saturday, I had to drive around the block 5 times to find a parking space! As a result, my children almost missed the beginning of Miss Sue's reading of the new Harry Potter book!

The problem is simple: the library has no parking space of its own. Instead, it shares a lot with the Bill's Hardware Store, the Baker's Dozen Mall, and Cozy's Diner! At this time of year, when everyone is out and about doing their Christmas shopping, there isn't an empty parking space to be found in all of downtown Elmhurst!

We must solve this problem soon, or someone is going to have to explain to my children why they can't go to Story Hour anymore!

Jane Rochester
Elmhurst

Pornographic Literature Taught at EHS

Parents, I'm here to warn you about a serious problem here in Elmhurst. Some of our own children are being forced to read and study pornography, right here in our tax supported high school. I'm referring to the novel *The Handmaid's Tale*, which is required reading for many of our Elmhurst seniors, including my daughter Mollie. In case you are unfamiliar with the novel, I will briefly explain it for you: *The Handmaid's Tale* is a futuristic tale of a woman who is forced to live with a family and bear their children, as the woman of the house is infertile.

Letters to the Editor

The novel is filled with various immoral sexual scenes, such as graphic description of two women in bed with a man at the same time. Furthermore, the book also discusses transvestitism and glorifies lesbianism. Issues such as rape and abortion are also mentioned.

The book is not only sexually explicit, it is a thinly veiled attack on Christianity and the religious right. It has often been referred to as a "feminist *1984*," and it is amoral feminist propaganda at its worst—or best, depending on your point of view. As a concerned parent and a Christian, I refuse to let my daughter be subjected to such filth, and I hope you make the same decision. Please contact our school immediately and ask them to remove this immoral novel from their curriculum! Let them know you care about our children!

Reverend John Albright
Elmhurst Community Church

(After these letters, Melanie included a church bulletin to portray the atmosphere of Rev. Albright's church. It can be found on the book's website *www.boyntoncook.com/multiplegenresmultiplevoices.*)

Letters to the Editor

Thank you for your concern!

I'd just like to thank everyone who visited me in the hospital when I was having my hip replaced. I would especially like to thank my next door neighbor, Velma Hayes, who stopped by everyday with her famous tuna noodle casserole. I would also like to thank my pastor, Rev. John Albright, for his numerous visits. Also, I can't forget to thank The Elmhurst Community Church Ladies Sewing Group for the beautiful lap robe. Your cards, prayers, and support have meant so much to me! I'm so lucky to live among such caring folks!

Bertha Mason
Elmhurst

Don't tolerate porn in Elmhurst!

I have just received news that Acme Adult Bookstores, Inc., is considering opening a new store on Rt. 17 just outside of Elmhurst. The store will be selling pornographic books, magazines, and videos. It is expected to open in mid–July.

We cannot continue to allow women to be denigrated and objectified by the porn industry. We must take a stand on this issue! Join us tonight at Elmhurst Community College for our annual Take Back the Night. At this event we will be circulating petitions against the Rt. 17 porn store. If we work together, we can keep porn out of Elmhurst!

Annie Kenyon
Elmhurst

Censorship at Elmhurst High School

As a senior at Elmhurst High School, I was appalled when I read Reverend John Albright's letter regarding *The Handmaid's Tale*, a novel that I had just finished studying in my English class. His accusations against the book were taken completely out of context. From his letter, it is apparent that he does not understand the novel at all—perhaps he has not even read the entire book.

In *The Handmaid's Tale*, author Margaret Atwood speaks of a society that is controlled by a fundamentalist religious group. The group controls the movements of all the citizens, including what materials—if any—they are permitted to read. While such a scenario seems far-fetched at first glance, I am writing to tell you Reverend Albright's actions prove that the same mentality that exists in Atwood's fictional Gilead is alive and well here in Elmhurst.

As Americans, our forefathers fought hard so that we could live in a free society. We cannot stand by and let anyone tell us what we should or should not be allowed to read. This country is filled with religious fanatics like Reverend Albright who spend their time imposing their moral standards on those around them.

Please contact the school immediately in support of the novel and of Ms. Allison Johnson, our English teacher. If we don't stand up and fight for our freedoms, we will lose them.

Bianca Montgomery
Elmhurst

(See the book's website *www.boyntoncook.com/multiplegenresmultiplevoices* for an excluded term paper on the religious conservatism in *The Handmaid's Tale* written by Bianca Montgomery, the same student who wrote this last letter to the editor.)

Elmhurst Public Library

120 Main St.
Elmhurst, Ohio 44719
555-3623

April 17, 2000

Reverend John Albright
Elmhurst Community Church
310 Main Street N.W.
Elmhurst, Ohio 44719

Reverend Albright:

Immediately following your request for reconsideration of Margaret Atwood's novel, *The Handmaid's Tale*, we formed a committee to review the novel. The committee was composed of myself and five other librarians or trustees of the library. Each of us carefully read *The Handmaid's Tale*, and we discussed the work at great length. We also searched our archives for reviews of the novel and read those as a group. We met on three different occasions to discuss this situation.

Upon our careful consideration of *The Handmaid's Tale*, we have decided to keep the book on our shelves. While the book does contain some portions that we admit could be offensive to some of our patrons, we do not consider the book to be pornographic or gratuitous in nature. Our research shows that our colleagues agree with us, as *Library Journal*, one of the foremost publications in our discipline, proclaimed that *The Handmaid's Tale* is "highly recommended for most libraries." We are confident that we have made the right decision in this matter.

Thank you for your interest in the collection of The Elmhurst Public Library. If you have any questions or would like to examine the minutes from our meetings about this matter, you are more than welcome to meet with me regarding our decision.

Sincerely,

Eliza Winthrop

Eliza Winthrop
Elmhurst Library Director

(See the book's website for an excluded email message, the final genre in the MVA, in which Mollie tells Sarah that her father has put her in a new school because the School Board supported Ms. Johnson. Melanie's References for this project and her "Rationale" are also included on the website.)